SHEFFIELD

in the age of the tram

This map clearly illustrates the extent of the Sheffield tramway system when it was still in full operation. No thoughts of abandonment had taken place – indeed, more new cars were to be delivered within the next two or three years. It seemed as though Sheffield planned to have an efficient and superbly maintained tramway for many years to come. The detailed and comprehensive map shows virtually every part of the system and will revive memories for many people.
Courtesy of John Gillham

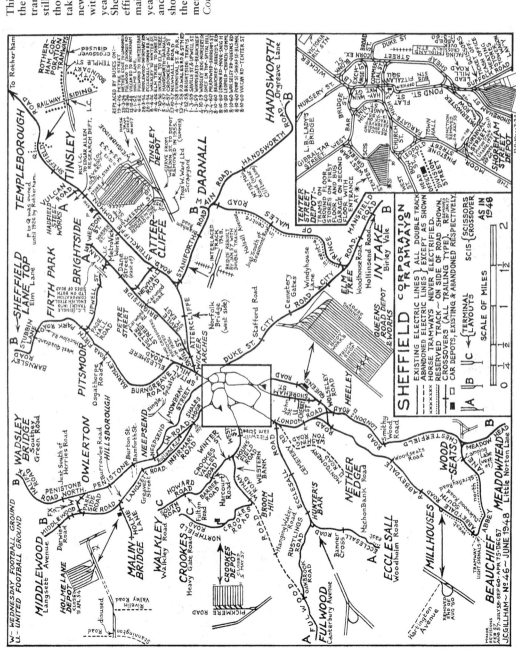

SHEFFIELD

in the age of the tram
1950-60

Graham H. E. Twidale

·THE NOSTALGIA OF BRITAIN·
from
The NOSTALGIA Collection

© Graham H. E. Twidale 1995 and 2004

First published in 1995 as *A Nostalgic Look at Sheffield Trams since 1950*

Reprinted in this format 2004

British Library Cataloguing in Publication Data

A catalogue record for this book is available from the British Library.

ISBN 1 85794 191 8

Silver Link Publishing Ltd
The Trundle
Ringstead Road
Great Addington
Kettering
Northants NN14 4BW

Tel/Fax: 01536 330588
email: sales@nostalgiacollection.com
Website:
www.nostalgiacollection.com

Printed and bound in Great Britain

A Silver Link book
from
The NOSTALGIA *Collection*

ACKNOWLEDGEMENTS

To compile a book of this nature obviously entails a great deal of research. This usually takes two forms. The first is the personal visits to reference libraries and locations where original photographs were taken, and the second, and probably the most important, is the help and assistance given by many people and organisations. This book is no exception.

Richard Wiseman was a tremendous source of help, both in the supply of information and the text reading he has done for me.

Keith Terry, together with Richard, supplied most of the superb negatives used in the book, together with others from the John Fozard collection and one or two from Steve Palmer.

My grateful thanks to Peter Skelton of Gloucester for his tremendous achievement in providing first-class prints from most of the historic black and white negatives.

I should also like to record my appreciation to the following organisations for valuable and interesting information, which, I hope, has gone to make up equally interesting captions to the photographs: Barclays Bank plc, TSB Bank plc, Yorkshire Bank plc, Gunstone's Bakery, C&A, Trebor Bassett Ltd, Sheffield United FC, Sheffield Wednesday FC, Joshua Tetley & Son, and the Aizlewood Business Centre. Finally, thanks are due to Peter Harvey of *The Star* for his helpful information and to my great friend and colleague Frank Whiley who took the present-day photographs while accompanying me on one of my many visits to the city.

BIBLIOGRAPHY

Hague, Graham, and Turner, Howard *Sheffield Trams Remembered*

Sheffield Cinema Society *The ABC of the Cinemas of Sheffield*

The Star, Images of Sheffield

Vickers, J. Edward *A Popular History of Sheffield*

Ward, Richard *In Memory of Sheffield Cinemas*

Halliwell's Film Guide

Memories of Sheffield – Its cathedral and parish churches

The Modern Tramway, various issues

CONTENTS

This superb shot of a very busy Fitzalan Square on Saturday 17 March 1956 shows Rocker panel car No 416, with only a short life in public service left, reversing on the Flat Street crossover prior to making her way back up to Wadsley Bridge, possibly at the same time picking up football supporters bound for Hillsborough. An Inspector nonchalantly surveys the scene as a cyclist hurries past anxious to get home after a morning's work.

The Bell Hotel was a familiar feature of the square for years, but Tetleys sold it in the early 1970s and it is now an amusement arcade. Next to the Bell can be seen the former Electra Palace Cinema, opened on 10 February 1911. Re-opened after the war as a News Theatre, it finally became the Classic on 15 January 1962. It closed on 24 February 1982, the victim of fire, and was subsequently demolished.

The smoke-blackened corner of the Head Post Office stands on the right. Opened in July 1910, it stood on the site of the former Queen's Cutlery works and replaced the former Head Post Office in Haymarket. The statue of Edward VII stares down Haymarket from his plinth, as, of course, he still does to this day. What a variety of scenes he has witnessed over the years – not only the bombing of December 1940, but also the bidding farewell to the first generation of trams and the welcoming of the second. *R. J. Wiseman*

INTRODUCTION

In 1986, when my great friend Nigel Harris decided to launch the 'Nostalgic look at...' series of books commencing with the trams in Glasgow, we little realised just how popular they would become. The Glasgow tram system was, perhaps, a bit special, and is still held in great affection by many Glaswegians who have never let it die. The series grew to a good many volumes, and is now being republished in this new format.

In the current volume we look at what was thought to be the last major street tramway system to run in England – Sheffield. I say 'thought to be' as it was inconceivable in 1960 that trams would ever appear again in the future, and yet in the 1990s a magnificent, brand-new integrated transport system was once more running in Steel City. The wheel really had turned full circle.

As in my other publications, I should stress that in absolutely no way is this book intended to be a definitive history of the Sheffield tramway system, nor for that matter the city in general. Others much more qualified than myself have authoritatively written specific publications on these subjects.

From its introduction on 6 October 1873,

Above left Standard car 148 turns into Staniforth Road from Attercliffe Road on 2 May 1957. The sharpness of the curve and the well-patched state of the road are clearly seen. Parked in Attercliffe Road is a Bedford van belonging to Abrafract of Sheffield, suppliers of grinding wheels, etc, to the famous local cutlery industry. Following the tram is a splendid removal van belonging to a Leeds firm. Further pictures of this junction will be found later in the book. *R. W. Wiseman*

Left Standard car No 135 pauses to pick up a passenger at the junction of Page Hall Road and Owler Lane on Thursday 27 June 1957. It is perhaps surprising that the only other vehicle in the scene is an ice-cream van.

As I have said about other similar photographs in other publications that I have compiled, this shot really typifies the 1950s with its familiar, homely shops, sunny days (it was always sunny then!), and far less stressed and hurried times. The age of the dreaded super/hypermarket had yet to appear and change our shopping habits for ever. The cast iron 'Keep Left' signs were much more robust items of street furniture than the plastic variety seen today and consequently lasted much longer. Save for a new roundabout system, the scene has today changed comparatively little. *R. J. Wiseman*

when the first horse tram clip-clopped from Lady's Bridge to the Golden Ball, Attercliffe, to the final closure almost 87 years to the day later on 8 October 1960, the system developed into one of the finest in the whole of the United Kingdom – but more of that in the History section.

How the Sheffield of the 1950s has changed since many of the photographs in this book were taken! From a thriving industrial city that played a premier role in the cutlery and silverware trade, and which resounded to the clang of the hammer and the heat of the furnaces in its heavy steel industry, it has seen an almost total revolution. The change has been dramatic, with whole industrial complexes and communities disappearing. Many famous names – Brown Bayley, Sandersons, Firth Browns, Cammells, Hadfields and George Senior, to name but a few – have all but disappeared. Wholesale demolition of factories and familiar works took place in the 1980s due to the decline in demand and competition, plus, I suspect, a sprinkling of politics.

On a recent visit to the city it was difficult to comprehend just how dramatic the changes have been, particularly around Attercliffe. When one has not been back to the area for some 30-odd years, it comes as something of a culture shock to try and remember what it had all looked like.

However, far from dying, the city has been reborn with newer industries taking over, and greater involvement in leisure activities. Many sites of former works now house totally different concepts in commercialism. Hadfields is, of course, the location of the now nationally known Meadowhall shopping complex, international sporting events take place at the Don Valley stadium where Brown Bayley carried on business, and the Ponds Forge name has been retained in the new swimming and leisure building as a reminder of George Senior, one of the city's most famous self-made men.

The city skyline has also changed considerably. Gone, for the most part, are the myriad factory chimneys, one or more of

On a quiet Sunday morning in February 1959 Roberts car No 508 climbs Waingate, with the Exchange Brewery and Lady's Bridge Hotel dominating the background. The brewery eventually became part of the Whitbread empire and survived until closure in 1994. The splendid blackened facades of the row of shops on the left stand out well with their fine architecture and neo-Roman porticos and balustrades. Although progress is inevitable, it is a pity that such fine buildings should have been swept away without much thought. Times, however, change and today more care and attention is given to similar examples of architecture that can be saved and refurbished. Readers may recall Colvin's and Broadmead, and also the Sheffield United booking office next door up the hill. *John Fozard collection*

At Vulcan Road terminus, the buildings of Hadfields steelworks dominate the scene. The location of this shot has now completely disappeared, all the buildings having been demolished and replaced by the new Meadowhall shopping complex. The last tram service to operate in the city ran from here to Millhouses or Beauchief, the final cars making the farewell journeys in public service on 8 October 1960.

Here we seem domed-roof Standard cars Nos 100, 274 and 280 in July 1956, with 100 pulling out into Sheffield Road on the long cross-city trip to Millhouses.

What a contrast these two termini made, with Vulcan Road deep in the heart of the industrial east end and suburban Millhouses and Beauchief in the south. Vulcan Road lay some 600 yards from Tinsley depot and the track was originally owned by Rotherham Corporation, but was transferred to Sheffield on New Year's Day 1926. Rotherham trams continued on the joint Sheffield service until December 1948, then on their own local route to Templeboro until November 1949. Vulcan Road sidings were laid in 1927. *John Fozard collection*

which accompanied every industrial site, and with them the black plumes of smoke and attendant steam that rose up from the many steelworks and forges.

Even the comparatively modern skyline has changed with, at the time, the much vaunted Park Hill and Hyde Park high-rise flats having now been either demolished or modified. Very much synonymous with the 1960s design thinking, the flats were a great source of pride to the city, as, of course, were other similar tower blocks then springing up all over the country. Subsequently this concept of housing design greatly lost its appeal and what, in some cases, had become a blight on the landscape were demolished. Even the 'Hole in the Road' has gone!

However, this book does not take us up to this period, but remains in the sort of time-warp that the 1940s and 1950s were. Comparatively speaking, little had changed since the war. Most people had jobs and lived in closely knit communities much as they and previous generations had done. The dramatic changes of the 1960s and 1970s had yet to rear their heads, when change for change's sake seemed to be the fashion and to be at the forefront of many people's minds. Many fine buildings were swept away in this period all over the country, but today, fortunately, wiser counsels prevail and much more thought is given to conservation, renovation and retention. The newly revitalised Victoria Quays complex is a fine example, and is a great credit to the City Council and the Sheffield Development Corporation.

This book is divided into various roughly delineated chapters ranging from city centre scenes to those on the outskirts, showing just how much of a contrast in outlook the city had to offer. For those old enough to remember the trams first time around, it will provide a chance to wallow in pure nostalgia. The scenes will be very familiar to you, as will the fashions, road vehicles, adverts on the hoardings and general background. It seems totally inconceivable that many of the pictures were captured on film some 50 years ago. Where has it all gone?

For younger readers it gives a historic chance to see how the city was in the bustling time of the 1950s, and how a fine and well-maintained tram fleet coped with the masses of people who still used public transport at that time. In 1951 the trams covered some 48 route miles in the city, carried 175,000,000 passengers and accounted for 64 per cent of all public transport traffic.

Look closely at the pictures and notice how many tram crews wore the full uniform with pride – even peaked caps! Notice also, for the most part, the absence of litter and graffiti, unlike today. The fast-food, throw-away society in which we now live causes Sheffield, and every other town and city in the United Kingdom, enormous problems in trying to keep on top of it. The mindless 'tagging' graffiti appearing all around the city today must sicken people of an older generation who never witnessed anything quite like it in former days.

A glance through the book's pages will for many, I am sure, rekindle fond memories of times past, bringing the sounds and sights almost to life. Remember the noise made by a procession of four-wheel trams rattling over the mass of rails at the junction of Fitzalan Square, Commercial Street, Haymarket and High Street; the squeal of protesting flanges as a car negotiated a particularly tight curve; and the warning gong that the driver hit with his foot to alert other traffic or pedestrians of the tram's presence, often accompanied by a verbal lashing!

Remember also taking the tram to Hillsborough or Bramall Lane for the football. Catching a tram for work, perhaps in the industrial east end or, in complete contrast, swaying down the grassed reservation on Abbey Lane on a fine summer's day with the Derbyshire hills in the background.

There are so many other remembrances and sounds to recall from those days. Perhaps lying in bed and hearing the last car of the night passing nearby on its way back to the depot, trolleywheel hissing on rain-soaked wires, while in the background the shrill whistle of an ex-Great Central freight locomotive crossing the city with a rake of coal wagons and the sounds of steam engines shunting loose-coupled wagons – I could go on waxing lyrical for ages!

There is so much to see and recall in the book's pages. One or two people are clearly

On a gloomy Saturday 6 October 1956 Roberts car No 504, on service to Woodseats, passes by the siding on Parkside Road used for football specials, where Standard cars 247 and 8 wait to head back to the city. The day was not all gloom, however, for Wednesday were at home to Sunderland and beat them 3-2 in front of a crowd of 33,000 with Broadbent, Shiner and Froggatt scoring. On the hoarding Miss Jubilee of 1956 proclaims 'Jubilee Stout suits me – you'll find it suits you too'. *A. K. Terry*

shown in several of the pictures. Who knows, it may be you or someone you knew who just happened to be passing by at the time and was, unwittingly, captured in the click of the shutter.

I have, in some cases, left a photograph's caption with little detail. Older residents of the city will be able to recognise and recall background scenes much better than I could ever hope to do.

So there you are. Wander off down Memory Lane recalling with affection the days when life was seemingly much less hurried and stressful, when children still played in the street and listened to Children's Hour on the wireless, people went to the pictures in their thousands or just sat in front of the cosy and warm open coal fire, so much a feature of the time and now, by and large, also a thing of the past.

Television was, comparatively, still in its infancy, and the wireless provided much of the home entertainment. Remember enjoying the comedy programmes *Life with the Lyons*, *The Huggetts*, *Ray's a Laugh*, *Take it from Here*, *Educating Archie*, and the late, great Al Read. Happy days! All these things are gone, never to return. But then, who would ever have imagined in their wildest dreams that trams would ever run in the streets of Sheffield again?

A BRIEF HISTORY OF SHEFFIELD TRAMWAYS

On the appallingly wet night of 8 October 1960, Sheffield said goodbye to its trams, which, in one form or another, had served the city for 87 years. At that time it was felt that it really was the end of an era and that the motor bus, which had replaced them, was here to stay. How incorrect those thoughts have turned out to be as current transport events have shown. However, more of that later.

It had all begun on 6 October 1873 when the city's first horse tramway opened from Lady's Bridge to the Golden Ball Hotel, Attercliffe. The Corporation owned the tramway but leased the track to the Sheffield Tramways Company. Prior to this there had been some horse bus services, but these tended to serve the more well-to-do parts of the city.

Horse tram routes eventually worked from Snig Hill to Hillsborough, and Moorhead to Heeley and Nether Edge, while an extension had been added to the original route, taking it to Tinsley and Brightside. The horse trams themselves were either single-deck cars drawn by one horse, or open-top double-deck cars drawn by two.

Trials were undertaken by a steam tram in January 1877 on the Brightside route (for one day only) and again in 1878, but citizens were not impressed by the dirt and smoke, and the experiment was short-lived.

In 1896, 20 years after the horse trams had commenced operation, the Corporation took over the Sheffield Tramways Company and by 5 September 1899 had opened the first electric route from Nether Edge to Tinsley. Receipts in the first year amounted to £30,000, but by 1908, with increased route miles, this had increased to an incredible £285,952.

Travelling in the early electric cars must have been quite a thrill with their comfortable ride and comparative speed. All the existing lines were eventually electrified except the full length of Weedon Street, which remained a terminal stub for electric cars at the Tinsley end until the final days of the system. The last horse tram ran on 11 November 1902.

The Victorians were slow to provide cheap available transport for the working classes, but a change of monarch soon altered this. By the time Edward VII died in 1910 there had been much expansion of the system, with 39 route miles being operated with 264 cars.

After the First World War the system continued to expand as the population grew and new housing estates were built. Extensions of existing track took place between Millhouses and Woodseats in April 1927, along Prince of Wales Road in 1928, and also to Meadowhead in the same year. The final extensions were to Handsworth and Sheffield Lane Top in 1934 and Intake in 1935. Earlier extensions had taken place up to Ecclesall and Fulwood in 1922 and 1923 respectively.

Since electrification a variety of cars, both single- and double-deck, had been built for the city, and due to the steepness of many hills and the abundance of sharp curves, all were four-wheeled; indeed, all cars built up until 1952 were of a single-truck arrangement. All the electric cars collected current from the overhead wires by means of a trolley with a swivel-head wheel arrangement. This enabled trams to use the many automatic trolley reversers that were a feature at every terminus and many crossovers throughout the city. The trolley reverser had first been introduced to the system in December 1915.

Many of the very early cars were eventually rebuilt from open-top to totally enclosed vehicles. Cravens of Darnall and the Corporation's own Queens Road Works were responsible for many of the trams running in the city streets. Other car builders included the United Car Company of Preston, Brush Engineering of Loughborough, and the North East company of W. E. Hill.

Most of the pictures in this book show predominantly three different types of car, which were represented right up until the final day. They were the Standards, straight-sided or flush-panelled (as against the earlier

The impatient driver in the Ford Consul is itching to overtake Standard car No 160 pictured here in fine weather on 12 April 1958 in the Wicker at the junction of Blonk Street. The Wicker was one of three places on the tramway system that had centre pole overhead wire supports, the others being on Prince of Wales Road and Abbey Lane.

By October 1958, No 160 was one of the last five cars to retain the old livery of Prussian blue and cream, and in this picture looks to be in fine condition. However, it would not see another 12 months in service before being withdrawn. *A. K. Terry*

'Rocker panel' cars), of which 211 were built between 1927 and 1936; the domed-roof Standards, 78 being constructed, included wartime rebuilds; and 36 modern cars, the precursor of which was constructed in Queens Road in 1946.

During the Second World War the trams really came into their own, providing an intensive service for industries that worked round the clock. During the terrible two nights' Blitz in December 1940 14 trams were destroyed, but all were rebuilt during the course of the war. Extra trams were purchased from Bradford and Newcastle to supplement and maintain the high level of service that was required.

A pleasant three-quarter view of Standard car No 3 outside Midland station on Sunday 1 May 1955 on a short working back to Walkley. Whereas Pepsi-Cola still thrives today, the backdrop to this scene has all vanished save for the station buildings. Even the once ubiquitous red K6-type telephone kiosks are now something of a rarity. Introduced in 1935 to a design by Sir Giles Gilbert Scott, they have largely been replaced with the modern, no doubt more cost-effective, efficient and vandal-proof yet soulless (and draughty) glass boxes. However, some red boxes remain in Sheffield and many other towns and cities – some of them are now listed 'buildings'. *A. K. Terry*

During the Second World War, Sheffield purchased 10 ex-Bradford and 14 ex-Newcastle Corporation trams to help maintain and supplement services needed for round-the-clock industrial production. Here is one of the Bradford cars, No 330, showing Crookes School Road on its destination blind; this was, of course, the location of the depot. Once withdrawn from public service, 330 had its top deck removed and became a rail grinder in the works fleet. She survived right until the end of tramway operation in the city and was ultimately preserved by the Tramway Museum Society and resides at Crich. *A. K. Terry*

In 1946 a completely revolutionary class of tramcar emerged from the works at Queens Road and was numbered 501. As this was exactly 50 years since the take-over of the Sheffield Tramways Company by the Corporation, the car was known as the Jubilee. Thirty-five other similar cars were built between 1950 and 1952 by Charles Roberts of Wakefield and were commonly referred to as the 'Roberts cars'. They were truly superb vehicles and were the latest thing in public transport luxury. They were, however, to be the tramway fleet's swansong.

Even before the last one, No 536, entered service on 11 April 1952, the City Council had taken the momentous decision to rid the city of its magnificent tramway system over a period of 15 years. In the event this turned out to be an over-estimation as everything was to vanish within eight years.

The livery of the Sheffield tram fleet, particularly for the purpose of this book, by and large remained in two schemes. The first was a rich dark Prussian blue and cream with gold lining, the later azure blue with a mainly all-over cream appearance.

It is said that in earlier times the tram fleet was given 20 coats of paint, which lasted them a lifetime except for touch-up and varnish. Indeed, many Standard cars saw their time out in the old Prussian blue and cream livery, the last one, No 199, being withdrawn from service on 1 March 1959, having been the last car to travel down Abbey Lane from Woodseats to Millhouses the previous evening.

While on the subject of liveries, at the Town Hall banquet given for invited guests on the evening of the final procession, the Transport Committee Chairman, Alderman Dyson,

This is one of the Newcastle cars, No 313, in Flat Street at a date unknown but thought to be 1950/51. After serving their purpose well and as a result of new Roberts cars coming off the production line, they were withdrawn from traffic in 1951. *John Fozard collection*

In 1952 an experimental livery was tried out on 23 cars, some being in an all-over unrelieved green and others, similar to Standard car No 150 shown here outside Shoreham Street depot, in a two-tone variety. Members of the Sheffield public, who had for so long been used to either dark Prussian blue and cream or the lighter azure blue and cream, were outraged and voiced strong disapproval. Fortunately the experiment was subsequently deemed to have been unsuccessful and all the cars were repainted back to their normal livery. *R. J. Wiseman*

explained in his speech why the city had adopted a mainly cream livery in the 1930s, whereas the tram and bus fleets of most industrial towns and cities were in much darker and sometimes drabber colours. The cream was deliberately adopted as a challenge and symbol of pride to enable the trams to stand out in the varying backgrounds of Sheffield and, presumably, to force maintenance staff to keep them extra-clean!

However, in 1952 a trial livery was chosen on 23 cars using either an unrelieved all-over green or with a two-tone variation. This, to say the least, did not go down at all well with Sheffield citizens, who were very vocal in their opposition. The scheme was ultimately withdrawn and all the offending cars were returned to their more familiar colours.

The real beginning of the end for Sheffield's trams started with the abandonment of the Ecclesall to Middlewood route in March 1954. Over the next six years all the remaining services would gradually disappear: the hilly and tortuous routes to Crookes and Walkley, those to Sheffield Lane Top, Woodseats or Meadowhead, Wadsley Bridge, up the fine reservation of Prince of Wales Road, around the heavily industrialised areas of the east end and, finally, the route from Millhouses or Beauchief to Vulcan Road – a total contrast in surroundings.

Two Robert cars, Nos 510 and 513, were

'When icicles hang by the wall' etc... A real winter's tale here on Crookes Road at the junction of Spooner Road. It is Tuesday 18 January 1955 and the snowfall of a day or two earlier has now been well compacted into the footpath, and melting snow, other than in the roadway where rivers of water pour down the grooved tramlines, has turned to ice. Two Standard cars head for Crookes, although No 143 appears to be heading for the depot, having come off the Firth Park service. *R. J. Wiseman*

specially painted for the last week of operations and took part, together with other cars of the class and preserved vehicles, in the final procession on a foul, wet night, Saturday 8 October 1960. Thousands turned out to witness the passing of an era, which was also the last major street tramway in England, Leeds having abandoned its tramway system a year earlier. Glasgow would keep the flag of St Andrew flying for a further two years before it, too, yielded up its huge system to the motor bus.

Trams had been held to be mainly responsible for the creation of traffic hold-ups in towns and cities and, despite the fact that they carried enormous numbers of passengers quickly, cheaply, efficiently and cleanly for many years, due to poor foresight and lack of forward thinking and planning they became something of an anathema to councils anxious to 'modernise' their transport undertakings with buses.

It is amazing that no lessons seemed to have been learned from the continent, where fleet modernisation had taken place and, together with tramway extensions on reserved track, had ensured their survival. Trams still, of course, run in many places in Europe to this day. Perhaps the prevailing attitude of the time exuded the 'Little Englander' theory that 'after all, we are British and really know best'.

Well, we have, in some cities, come full circle in the tramway experience. Manchester led the way with the introduction in 1992 of its modern tramway system, the Metrolink, which joined the towns of Altrincham and Bury; although most of the track is on former stretches of railway track, new street track was to appear in the city centre for the first time since 1949.

Sheffield first thought of the re-introduction of a tramway system back in 1979, with a technical evaluation in 1984/85. This later culminated in the exciting and inspiring Supertram project, linking Meadowhall and Hillsborough and the city centre to Gleadless and Birley. No one who witnessed the final procession of the first system in 1960 would in their wildest imaginings have ever believed they would, 34 years later, be seeing trams once more running up Commercial Street and High Street.

This is only the briefest of brief glimpses at the history of the Sheffield tram and its development, the merest insight into something that has been well documented by others – it is designed just to whet the reader's appetite.

THE CITY CENTRE

This view on Saturday 4 May 1957 at Fitzalan Square junction shows the mass of rail and overhead wires that were a major feature here for many years. Domed-roof Standard car No 265 clatters over the various crossings on its way to Crookes. This was the last day that trams would operate to the highest point on the system, reaching some 729 feet. A Ford Prefect, Standard 8 and Austin Cambridge further animate the scene as an Inspector waits to board the car from which this photo was taken.

The splendid blackened facade of Barclays Bank stands out well in the right background. Built in the late 19th century, it formerly housed the Midland Counties Bank before Barclays took over. It closed for business on Friday 5 September 1969, moving to new premises further down Commercial Street, which commenced trading the following Monday. Unfortunately the old building suffered the fate of so many around this time and was soon to be demolished. Some years later, during redevelopment, workmen digging found an old safe and several filing cabinets buried below ground. Perhaps the contents solved many a problem of where missing items had got to in the bank's earlier move! *A. K. Terry*

Above On the opposite corner of Commercial Street and Haymarket in Fitzalan Square stands the solid edifice of the Yorkshire Penny Bank. The building originally housed the Post Office and was opened in 1872. When the new Head Post Office opened in Fitzalan Square on 4 July 1910 the Stock Exchange took over part of the premises. The Yorkshire Penny Bank moved into the building on 7 May 1926 and purchased the former Stock Exchange in 1968 for expansion. It still stands today, albeit in a much cleaner state, as the Yorkshire Bank plc (the Penny having been 'dropped' during the Bank's centenary year in 1959).

This was a very busy tramway junction and here we see Roberts car No 512 and Standard car No 266 crossing each other's path at right angles. The noise for people working in the bank and the Road Transport & General Insurance Co Ltd must have been quite something, particularly as double glazing on the scale it is used today was almost unheard of.

F. W. Woolworth, seen in Haymarket, was to move further down the thoroughfare to a new building on the site of the old Norfolk Market. *R. J. Wiseman*

Above right A busy Friday afternoon in High Street on 24 July 1959, giving a broader view of the two buildings mentioned above. That year was, by and large, a superb summer with long, hot sunny days, but 24 July must have been an exception. Three trams are captured from the top

deck of the one following Roberts car No 519, which has paused to pick up a lengthy queue of passengers from the loading island. The conductor has forgotten to change the indicator from Beauchief to, presumably, Vulcan Road. Domed-roof car No 264, which was later to survive scrapping and be preserved at Crich, pulls up the incline bound for Woodseats, while an unidentified Roberts car prepares to cross from Fitzalan Square into Haymarket.

A wonderful array of Ford, Austin and Morris cars completes the scene, which, on the left at least, remains much the same today. Although Barclays Bank was demolished around 1969/70, the cinema next to it would survive until 24 November 1982. *Steve Palmer*

Right A sunnier Saturday 12 April 1958 was yet another last day in the history of the city's tramways; at 11.15pm that night the last tram would leave Fitzalan Square bound for Darnall, Prince of Wales Road and Elm Tree. Here, earlier in the day, we see Standard car No 244 about to reverse and head back to Darnall.

Three boys, with suitably greased 'Elvis' hair-dos, cross the zebra crossing; the lad on the right, seemingly timid, grasps his companion's coat tail. The building in the right background has been sold and is shortly to re-open as a branch of Wigfalls. It has since been demolished and the site redeveloped. *R. J. Wiseman*

Above left Looking now into Fitzalan Square towards High Street, we see a busy scene with the then familiar sight of a white-coated and armbanded policeman on point duty at the junction. Immaculate Roberts car No 526 rocks over the junction on the last day of the service from Crookes to Handsworth, 4 May 1957.

The large board to the left behind 526 is headed 'Sheffield Savings Committee'. Savings Committees like this were nationwide at this time and were part of the National Savings movement. They were formed to encourage the savings habit and, although unreadable in this shot, the board must have been giving results of savings drives within the city.

The remains of the Marples Hotel can be quite clearly seen a little further to the left. This was a seven-storey building that received a direct hit during enemy action on Thursday 12 December 1940. The building was totally destroyed, killing between 60 and 70 people. *John Fozard collection*

Left Standard car No 113, with only a few weeks of service left, passes by the shattered remains of Burton's store on the corner of Angel Street and High Street in April 1957. Both Burton's and the adjoining C&A store were destroyed in the bombing of December 1940; after the war C&A opened a two-storey shop (due to post-war building restrictions) on 22 September 1952. The remaining four floors were added in 1954. The shell of Burton's remained for many years before being demolished and replaced with new development. Waring & Gillow were one-time occupants, but C&A later took over the whole complex.

C&A (it stood for Clemens & August Brenninkmeyer, two Dutch businessmen from a well-known family) opened their first store in Holland in 1841. The first store to open in the United Kingdom was in Oxford Street, London, in 1922. The Sheffield store was built on the site of the old Fitzalan Market and opened with great ceremony on Friday 18 March 1932 with a bumper sale. A full-page advert in the previous evening's *Yorkshire Telegraph and Star* showed a wide variety of bargains to be had ranging from 'one of the newest coat frocks with tasteful contrast trimmings and a box pleated skirt at 24s 11d', to 'a two-piece suit, beautifully tailored and designed on a self-knopped fancy material with a smartly fitting jacket and simply lovely frock at 3½ gns'. *John Fozard collection*

Above On a busy Saturday afternoon, 23 March 1956, crowds throng High Street, particularly around C&A. Standard car No 158 is turning into Haymarket on its way to Vulcan Road, while four other cars make their way up High Street, No 127 at the rear.

Walsh's store can be seen on the left looking still quite new, having only opened in May 1953. John Walsh opened his first store on this site in 1899 but this was another building destroyed in the Blitz of December 1940. The store seen here subsequently became Rackhams and later House of Fraser.

The scene is very reminiscent of an age when public transport was still heavily used; multi-storey car parks and parking meters had yet to appear and the use of private cars was on nothing like the scale it is today. *A. K. Terry*

Left Crowds thronged the streets of Sheffield for a different reason on Saturday 18 April 1953 – Princess Margaret was making a visit to the city prior to the Coronation of her sister less than two months away. There seem to be plenty of special policemen and St John's Ambulance men in evidence here at the junction of High Street and Fargate. An elderly Sergeant holds back a mother and child from crossing in front of the Austin Devon, which, in turn, is passing Rocker panel car No 377 on its way to Hunters Bar. The shattered remains of Burton's can again be seen, with C&A still to be rebuilt. In view of the Royal Visit it is perhaps a little surprising that more flags and bunting are not in evidence. *R. J. Wiseman*

Below left A dull day in April 1957 sees Standard car No 191 about to turn into High Street from Fargate with the fine Sheffield Telegraph building dominating the background. Built around 1914/15, it replaced a smaller and older building from which the *Sheffield Telegraph* and *Star* were published. Sheffield Newspapers moved out of the front offices and shops in 1960 when new works were opened at the back of the site, and a new front entrance was set up in York Street. Known as Kemsley House for many years, the building survives today but is used by a variety of businesses. *John Fozard collection*

In a pleasant scene at the junction of Church Street, High Street and Fargate on the last day of the Walkley-Intake service, domed-roof Standard car No 303 is on a short working to Midland station. Despite the surroundings having changed little, it is quite incredible that almost 50 years after this photo was taken, trams are once more making their way up Church Street. *R. J. Wiseman*

Above left Again, it is difficult to imagine that trams would one day again be running past this spot; wartime rebuild car No 201 negotiates the Leopold Street, Church Street and West Street junction and heads towards Crookes on Tuesday 30 April 1957. The following Saturday night would see the end of the Crookes-Handsworth service and that, it was thought, was that – trams would never again be seen in this location. But miracles do happen! *R. J. Wiseman*

Left It is a warm and sunny 7 July 1955 on West Street as immaculate Standard car No 128 approaches the junction with Leopold Street on its way to Intake. The advert on the side of the tram proclaims that the aptly named Joseph

Fox is Sheffield's leading furrier. Furs were still a popular fashion item at that time – they'd never get away with it today! Notice also the little Friar Tuck 'Hole in the Wall' shop behind the girls crossing on the zebra. This fine building was subsequently demolished and has been replaced with a modern development. *R. J. Wiseman*

Above Standard car No 268 swings out of West Street into Leopold Street having left Crookes Depot a few minutes earlier to take up duty on the Millhouses service. Martins Bank was later taken over by Barclays and the building behind No 268, Steel City House, subsequently underwent major refurbishment. *A. K. Terry*

Standard car No 178 pauses in Leopold Street on 4 May 1957, presumably just having travelled down from Crookes depot to take up service on the Firth Park via Pitsmoor route. This was the final day that Crookes depot would operate, and No 178 was withdrawn soon after this shot was taken.

A variety of period cars make up the scene including Ford Consuls and Zephyr, Morris Minor and Hillman. In the left background is a sign pointing to the Playhouse. This theatre, the home of the Sheffield Repertory Company, was situated on Townhead Street and was highly successful over the years, helping many actors and actresses to launch their careers. It ultimately closed its doors and was replaced by the Crucible in 1971. *R. J. Wiseman*

Pinstone Street basks in fine weather on Tuesday 30 April 1957 as Standard car No 165 pulls into the kerbside to pick up passengers on its way to Meadowhead. Pinstone Street was unique in having a three-track layout, the middle rails being used by Ecclesall cars, which did not pick up at this point. After the closure of this route the line was left in situ as it was a handy method of overtaking for cars that were running late or out of schedule. The kerbside rails had been laid in September 1933.

The small girl and her mother stare down at the cameraman from the top deck, while the gentleman on the right, complete with gabardine raincoat and trilby, completes the 1950s scene. Apart from the tramlines and shelter (the latter remained in use for many years long after the trams had gone), little has changed here, with the buildings on the left remaining although with a change of ownership. *R. J. Wiseman*

Above left A splendidly animated scene on the (in)famous occasion of the Queen Mother's visit to the city on 17 May 1958. I quote from *The New Statesman and Nation* for 24 May: 'The danger of the Queen Mother's high-heeled shoes catching in the tram lines outside Sheffield Town Hall posed a problem for Corporation engineers recently. But they soon hit on a solution. They diverted the city's trams for two hours and laid tarmac across the lines.' The mayhem that ensued can well be imagined. One doubts that a possible problem with Royal shoes would result in expensive chaos today!

Here we see part of the transport undertaking's problem, with Standard car No 199 in Furnival Street having its trolley turned round manually in order that it could return to The Moor via Moorhead. As can be seen here, this was the limit of operation along Furnival Street, the through line from Sheaf Street having been last used on 4 January 1958. *R. J. Wiseman*

Left Here is a view of the city that today is totally unrecognisable. It is Monday 6 October 1958, the day after the new roundabout was introduced at the foot of The Moor and its junction with Ecclesall Road, which technically enhanced the reserved track on the tramway system by 100 yards! Standard car No 160, oblivious to the new requirements of the traffic system, passes through the centre with unidentifiable indicator blinds. *R. J. Wiseman*

Above Roberts car No 507 is captured in Flat Street bound for Woodseats on a bright, sunny day in March 1958. The Odeon Cinema in the background had opened less than two years earlier on 15 July 1956. It closed its doors as a cinema on 5 June 1971 and became a bingo establishment; however, the Odeon re-established itself further down the street shortly thereafter. The wonderful array of adverts on the hoardings speak for themselves, with a bar of Cadbury's Whole Nut at 7d. *John Fozard collection*

There is no mistaking the time of year when this shot was taken – the daffodils are in full bloom on 8 April 1957 as Standard car No 126 heads into Pond Street bound for Woodseats. Extension work to the Head Post Office can be seen on the left, while today a new sorting office complex has replaced the buildings on the right. The daffodils have also long gone, again replaced by modern development. *A. K. Terry*

Although looking in quite a decent state, Standard car No 23 is on her last journey to Weedon Street after being withdrawn from service. It is 4 May 1957 and the last trams to run between Crookes and Handsworth will shortly make their farewell journeys. As each route was abandoned the opportunity was taken to withdraw some of the older cars or those involved in accidents.

Compare this scene with the photograph on page 116 taken some seven years earlier. Major development has yet to take place, although St Luke's Church has disappeared from the skyline. The scene today is dramatically changed, with the Nelson Mandela students' building taking up much of the foreground. *R. J. Wiseman*

Above left Although not visible from this spot today, St John's Church spire and the railway station are the only items left recognisable in a scene much changed from this shot dated Sunday 24 March 1957, as Standard car No 107 rattles over the junction outside Shoreham Street depot on her way to Wadsley Bridge. A fine example of a scissors crossover appears in the foreground, with a general maze of rails and the web of the overhead. Shoreham Street depot was closed to trams on 1 March 1959 but survives, just, as a bus garage.

Note the gentleman on the right practising the time-honoured tradition of swinging the starting handle of his van, which has obviously failed to leap into life by the much easier method of the starter motor. Starting handles may have been a pain (and they could be brutes, even breaking your thumb if you were not careful to remove your hand quickly), but they certainly were a useful part of 1950s motoring. *R. J. Wiseman*

Left On a dull, cold day in March 1956, domed-roof Standard car 240 ambles down Commercial Street and prepares to pick up passengers at one of the two stepped shelters that served routes to Intake and Handsworth. Two small girls are deep in conversation, while the elderly gentleman watches the world go by.

The buildings on the left are long gone with the 'new' Barclays Bank complex now close by. A coal lorry, so very familiar at this time, grinds up the hill past the adverts for Guinness, Gas and Kodak film. Semprini, who was a popular and much-loved pianist for many, many years, is appearing at the City Hall. Gabardine macs are much in evidence, while the gentleman second from the left is carrying a brown paper carrier bag, much in use before the advent of today's plastic variety. *John Fozard collection*

Above The line connecting Sheaf Street and Pond Street to Moorhead was used fairly infrequently, comparatively speaking, and mainly at rush hours. Unsuspecting motorists, seeing what appeared to be unused track, frequently caused hold-ups as seen in this picture, where cars 3 and 109 have come to a standstill. The driver of the former has gone into Kennings to try and locate the owner of the Hillman van, no doubt accompanied by a verbal lashing!

This section of the system was fairly tortuous and partly single track, and much of it has now been swallowed up in redevelopment. However, the buildings shown here in Brown Street and Paternoster Row survive, although Kennings, together with the accompanying gas lamps, have departed. The track was last used on Saturday 4 January 1958. *A. K. Terry*

The blackened edifice of the Sheffield United Gaslight Company, built in 1874, looks down on Commercial Street on 28 April 1957 as Standard car 235 and Roberts car 507 pass by on the way to Handsworth and Crookes respectively. The Gas offices were built one year after the first horse tram ran in the city from Lady's Bridge to Newhall Road, Attercliffe. No one could have imagined that the offices would outlive one tram system almost from start to finish, then witness the start of another.

Today the building enjoys protected status with Grade 2 listing. The smoke-blackened facade has been cleaned, as have the other buildings in the background, showing off their architectural splendour to great effect. In the present-day equivalent view, taken on 14 November 1994, one of the new Supertrams heads up the incline to cross the bow-string bridge to Meadowhall. *A. K. Terry/Frank Whiley*

The clock shows 12.38pm on a dull Sunday 23 May 1954, with a smoke haze drifting across the background. Cars 78 and 530, the former bound for Intake, have both paused to pick up passengers. Note the two small boys in short trousers, blue and fawn gabardine macs and the then familiar school caps. How today's children would react to having to wear such similar apparel is easy to guess!

The panoramic vista of 1954 has changed so dramatically over the years with only the spire of St John's church, which can just be glimpsed between the building on the left and the flats in the background, being the only structure linking these two views. Everything else has been swept away during redevelopment. It is almost inconceivable that once more trams are running up Commercial Street, although a little higher off the ground than cars 78 and 530. *R. J. Wiseman/Frank Whiley*

This fine three-quarter view of Standard No 103 shows the elaborately lined-out livery of Prussian blue and cream, as the tram turns from Sheaf Street into Commercial Street, with the Ford depot of Sheaf Street Motors in the background; a new Ford Consul can be glimpsed through the showroom window. Again all this area has completely disappeared and is dominated by the Park roundabout, although trams today run near this spot, albeit several feet above ground level! *A. K. Terry*

In an animated scene taken on a sunny Sunday morning in April 1957, the track gang are busy re-laying rails at the junction of Sheaf Street and Broad Street. The pointwork and junction here had become redundant when trams running up Duke Street and City Road to Manor Top ceased on 7 April 1956. The Craven-bodied single-deck 1933 Leyland bus on the left was used for many years by permanent way gangs and was a familiar sight around the city.

Notice the two men in white coats and gloves directing motor traffic around the workings while domed-roof Standard car No 235, on its way to Handsworth, pauses to await the all-clear to proceed. *A. K. Terry*

Above left A perhaps uncharacteristic presence of litter appears in this scene as Standard car No 288 swings from Broad Street into Duke Street on Saturday 7 April 1956. This would be the final day of operation for trams from Walkley to Intake via Duke Street and City Road as well as the Darnall circular service – up to Manor Top and down Prince of Wales Road.

The pinnacles of the former Corn Exchange can be seen in the background, while a postman, or more likely a telegraph boy, bounces along the setts on his bicycle – the latter seemingly still the same type used today! Boots the Chemist advertises that 'National Health prescriptions are dispensed here', no doubt free at that time... Meanwhile British Railways are offering excursions to Tissington Well Dressing and day returns to Manchester for 8s 9d (3rd Class) and 13s 3d (1st Class). Finally, a Leyland PD2 bus and a soft-top Hillman complete a scene that today is totally unrecognisable. R. J. Wiseman

Left Another scene that is also now completely unrecognisable is the junction of Blonk Street, Sheaf Street and Exchange Street, seen here on Saturday 4 May 1957. Standard car 125 was a Shoreham Street depot car, and on this day, the last of the Crookes-Handsworth service, it was withdrawn, together with many other similar cars. Here we see 125 making her final journey to Tinsley where, across the road from the depot, she was broken up in Ward's yard on 22 July 1957.

On the right Roberts car No 523 heads up Exchange Street on the Sheffield Lane Top via Attercliffe and New Hall Road service. This last ran on 26 October 1957 when Exchange Street was closed to trams. The street loop had also been formerly used by Rotherham trams until they ceased running on 12 December 1948.

The background is dominated by the Old Corn Exchange building, which was erected by the Duke of Norfolk in 1881, but which was gutted by fire in 1947 but survived as a ruin, as seen here, until 1964. It stood opposite the Fruit Market where a van is parked advertising 'Elasto Tablets' for 'My poor legs'. What on earth the tablets were supposed to do or indeed contained is unknown. R. J. Wiseman

Above It's 12 April 1958 as Standard car No 204 swings into Haymarket past John Collier, 'the Window to Watch', on the left. Formerly the premises had been part of the Fifty Shilling Tailor group of shops, originally conceived by Sir Henry Price in 1928 whereby men could buy a suit incorporating the best of tailoring standards and value, all at a price of 50 shillings – £2 10s. The business thrived, although after the war the title became something of a misnomer. When Sir Henry retired in 1954 he was succeeded as Chairman by John Collier, and his fellow Directors agreed to adopt his name for the new company. This eventually became part of the Burton empire. Today the corner is occupied by the Halifax Building Society. A. K. Terry

Above left At the same location as the previous photograph, Standard car No 150, built in 1930 by the North East company W. E. Hill, rattles over the multiplicity of rails into Haymarket on Saturday 12 April 1958 while the policeman on point duty pauses for a moment with his hands behind his back. Anyone doing this same job today would probably need to wear a mask to save themselves from carbon monoxide poisoning! Car 150 looks a little weary with a dent in its dash end and its lower indicator blind glass swinging free.

The tall crane in the background seems to be preparing the site for the new Castle Market, while the old Norfolk Market, seen to the right of the crane, will close down in 1959. *R. J. Wiseman*

Left This fine panoramic view of Waingate, the Exchange Brewery, the Lady's Bridge Hotel, tram-replacement buses, the splendid row of shops on the left and Roberts car No 511, was taken from the top deck of a tram

travelling the opposite way on Friday 24 July 1959. The shops have long since gone but the brewery and hotel remain, although no longer in operation. *Steve Palmer*

Above A small boy peeps through the railings down to the River Don on a warm, sunny day in September 1953 as Standard car No 117 crosses historic Lady's Bridge on her way to Darnall and up to Elm Tree, Intake. Remarkably, all the buildings in the picture survive. Williams Deacon's Bank subsequently became Williams & Glynns Bank before being taken over by the Royal Bank of Scotland; the branch shown here is now closed.

The building in the centre background looks to be in a poor state. Duncan Gilmour 'Windsor Ales' are advertised on the wall of the Lion Hotel; this ultimately became part of the Tetley empire and the building was subsequently refurbished. Today it is no longer the Lion Hotel but the Grosvenor Guest House. *John Fozard collection*

Above Here is a scene that, other than refurbishment, has changed very little over the ensuing years – the triangular junction of the Wicker and Blonk Street. It is Friday 3 May 1957 and Standard car No 243 turns into Blonk Street and heads for Crookes on the penultimate day of operation. The track and roadway look in remarkably good condition. This junction was in use right up until the end of the tram system on 8 October 1960. Blonk Street was a useful avoiding line for works access and football specials to Bramall Lane.

The Big Gun Hotel on the left survives, whereas Schweitzer's is now offices. Note the RAC road signs on the traffic light pole and the British Railways arrow pointing to 'Stations'; both Victoria and Midland were still in full swing at this time. *R. J. Wiseman*

Above right On another glorious sunny August day in the long hot summer of 1959 domed-roof car No 483 crosses over the same junction on her way to Beauchief. The fine Samuel Osborn building was demolished in about 1988, but the company name lives on today, albeit in a much reduced capacity. The splendid pre-war Ford completes an idyllic warm summer's afternoon scene. *John Fozard collection*

Right Although a tram, Standard car No 69, only just creeps into the picture, this is such a good shot of part of the Wicker cinema that I felt it had to be included, not to mention the new Bedford van and Ford Consul. The Wicker Picture House opened on 14 June 1920, being one of the most modern in the city at that time with electrically controlled curtains and air-conditioning. When partially completed in 1916 it had been requisitioned by the Ministry of Munitions.

The first film shown was entitled *Broken Blossoms* and starred Lillian Gish and Richard Barthelmess. As the film was set in China, usherettes were dressed in Chinese costumes and went up and down the isles swinging incense! Later in its life, as shown here, it showed the more lurid 'Sizzling Double X Programmes' – all good sex, violence and horror. Diana Dors was star billing this particular week in August 1959 in *Passport to Shame*; made in 1959 it also starred Herbert Lom and Eddie Constantine and revolved around a seamy melodrama with a taxi driver rescuing his girl from white slavery! 'Horrors from the Black Museum', meanwhile, was described as a crude shocker and starred Shirley Ann Field, Michael Gough and Geoffrey Keen. From 1962 the cinema became various 'Studios' before finally closing on 20 August 1987. It was then demolished and has been replaced by modern development.

The adjoining properties – Roberts Office Furniture, the Wicker Sweet Store (selling Dixon's mint rock) and Hallatts 'Transport House' and 'Cosy Café' have all gone, and presumably, after getting 'that sinking feeling', so too has the Titanic Steel Co. However, the large building above the tram's roof survives, as do, remarkably, most of the tall chimney pots, this being part of the existing NatWest Bank. *John Fozard collection*

In this classic scene at the Wicker arches on a busy Saturday 12 April 1958, three classes of tram are about to pass underneath, with domed-roof Standard car No 237 bringing up the rear. Above them is a fine example of an ex-Great Central Railway 'D11' 'Director' Class locomotive. These engines were designed by J. G. Robinson, the company's Chief Mechanical Engineer, in 1920, and were a regular feature around the Manchester and Sheffield area until the late 1950s. They were all named, with some bearing First World War battle locations such as *Ypres*, *Somme*, *Marne* and *Jutland*. The first member of the class, under British Railways numbering, was named *Butler-Henderson*, who was a Great Central Director and son of Alexander Henderson, later Lord Faringdon, who held the Chairmanship of the Great Central Railway and later became Deputy Chairman of the LNER. The engine survived the cutter's torch to become part of the National Collection based at the National Railway Museum in York.

The Wicker bridge was built in 1848 by Sir John Fowler to connect the Manchester, Sheffield & Lincolnshire Railway from Bridgehouses. Palmer & Harvey, tobacco and confectioner wholesalers, were a familiar feature at this time; the company still exists today although not in this location. *A. K. Terry*

The Wicker arches perfectly frame domed-roof Standard car No 233, which passes beneath on her way to Pitsmoor. Although just over a year has passed by since the previous photograph, locomotive power has changed and would continue to do so at an ever-increasing rate. Here we glimpse what appears to be an English Electric Type 4 diesel-electric locomotive (late Class 40), introduced in 1958, about to depart from Victoria station. The station closed in 1970 and the line to Manchester via Woodhead carried only freight until its closure. Perhaps in future years people in power may come to realise what a nonsensical notion it was to shut a modern electrified line serving the two great cities of Manchester and Sheffield with connections onward via Nottingham and Leicester to London.

Fortunately the Wicker arches survive as a Grade 2 listed structure and, now in a cleaner condition, stand as a proud memorial to the Great Central Railway and to a time of railway might. *John Fozard collection*

THE INNER CITY

Above This splendid three-quarter view shows Standard car No 213 turning out of Upwell Street into Brightside Lane at Hawke Street on Monday 1 July 1957 on its way to Darnall and Intake, Elm Tree. Although the car looks in very good condition, it has less than a year to go before withdrawal in April 1958. Note the tasteful way that adverts were applied to the sides of trams at this time. Note also the 'ship's wheel' handbrake on the driver's platform. Sheffield had a well-deserved reputation for keeping its trams and system generally in first-class order, and this photograph shows this certainly to be the case; No 213 stands out extremely well against the drab surroundings of the city's industrial heartland.

The newsagent and tobacconist on the right typifies many small shops abounding in the city in the 1950s; adverts for all sorts of items ranging from Craven 'A' and Robin cigarettes to the popular magazine *Illustrated* practically cover the entire facade of the shop. *Illustrated* was one of four major magazines on sale at this time – remember *Picture Post*, *Everybody's* and *John Bull*? All long gone of course. *R. J. Wiseman*

Above right A superb view of Roberts car No 508 as she turns from Attercliffe Road into Staniforth Road on 30 March 1958 – just 12 days to go before abandonment of the service up to Elm Tree, Intake. This was always a busy tramway junction until the closure of first the Crookes-Handsworth route on 4 May 1957, then the ending of the above-mentioned service. The junction certainly looks well worn by this date, as does the general state of the road.

The side panel advert on No 508 advertises 'Gunstone's Biscuits'. William Gunstone first opened a provision shop in Sheffield in 1862, and the company prospered through

his hard work and diligence to become a large wholesale business and a limited company in 1897. Pies, sausages and cooked meats were the main products until after the First World War, when expansion took the company into production of bread, biscuits and confectionery. The company moved to a purpose-built factory in Dronfield in 1951, and in 1972 Gunstone's became part of the Northern Food Group of companies.

A major fire in 1989 destroyed a large part of the factory, but a multi-million-pound investment saw the premises rebuilt and Gunstone's is today one of the largest factories in the area employing some 1,300 people, making a variety of comestibles all of which are supplied to the leading High Street stores.

The Burton's building in the right background of the picture was a part of a once busy and thriving shopping thoroughfare, which is now but a shadow of its former self. *A. K. Terry*

Right If most of the photographs in this book are to be believed, Sheffield was bathed in permanent sunshine in the 1950s! Here is a fine Sunday 28 April 1957 at the same junction, as 1934-built Standard car No 183 rocks over the junction complete with totally unreadable destination blinds. No 183 was a survivor, seeing service right until the very last day of tramway operation on 8 October 1960.

The shops on the right-hand side include Gallons Ltd ('Service, Quality, Economy'), where bacon has been reduced, Danish butter is 2s 10d and steak (presumably the tinned variety) is 1s 9d. Something has attracted a gathering of people further down the road outside the B&J Plant showrooms – surely they weren't Sunday trading! *A. K. Terry*

It is Sunday 29 September 1953, and the two young girls outside Frank Gregson's shoe shop look to be in their Sunday best, one of them clutching a bunch of flowers. Perhaps they are returning from Sunday School, something quite common 40 years ago but now, alas, much declined. Standard car No 125 rattles over the pointwork at the Main Road spur, Darnall, city-bound to Fitzalan Square. It is still in its original, fully lined-out livery of Prussian blue and cream. Grocer Burgon & Son and baker W. A. Broom were well-known names in the city at this time. *R. J. Wiseman*

Moving round to the south of the inner city, we see Standard car No 115 reversing on Shoreham Street by the Arnold Laver timber yard. It is Monday 8 July 1957, and presumably because it is outside the football season No 115 is on a cricket special. The tram had been built in 1932 and had a lower-deck rebuild some years later. It also lasted right until the final day of operation.

Bramall Lane was the home of Yorkshire County Cricket in the city until August 1973 when the final match, coincidentally between the great rivals Lancashire and Yorkshire, was played. As matches go it seems to have been fairly uninspiring; it certainly was a bowler's wicket, Yorkshire being skittled out for 99 in the first innings. Lancashire fared no better and declared at 111 for 8 wickets to try and make a match of it. It subsequently petered out into a draw.

Note the planks of wood precariously overhanging the pavement by the lamp-post on the left. Today, with health and safety regulations of paramount importance, they'd never get away with it. *A. K. Terry*

Above On a bitterly cold Wednesday 19 January 1955, Standard car No 194 pauses outside Highfield Library, London Road. The tram is about to turn right at the junction and head off down Abbeydale Road to Millhouses. In just over two years' time, No 194 will become the last car to leave Crookes when the route is abandoned on 4 May 1957 (although she did not leave Crookes until 1.30am on the 5th).

Note the impatient driver of the Austin Devon and the tram driver's observance of this action through his rear-view mirror. The small bread delivery van on the left is also noteworthy; this was at a time when van-to-door deliveries were still common, now very much a thing of the past. *R. J. Wiseman*

Above right Two months later, at 2pm on Saturday 12 March 1955, it is still perishing cold! The elderly gentleman on the left is well wrapped up against the chill as Standard car No 15 picks up passengers on London Road at the junction of Broadfield Road.

The Outsize Shop on the left would probably not be accepted as being 'politically correct' today, while Wainwrights seem to have everything for home furnishing – bedding, curtains, carpets, etc. Above John Mace's pet shop was the no doubt dubious Billiard Hall where much mis-spending of youth went on! *R. J. Wiseman*

Right We now find ourselves in the west of the inner city. It is Saturday 7 April 1956, the last day that the Walkley-

Intake tram service would operate. Here we have a never-to-be-repeated scene with four trams in sight, including Nos 276 and 72 and a classic shot of the pointsman, whose unique job on the system would cease after today.

Most tramway junctions were operated electrically by trolleys passing under a mechanism in the overhead. Generally speaking, if a car was going straight ahead it would coast towards the junction. If it was turning right or left, two notches of power would be applied by the driver. However, at this point on the system, at the junction of Houndsfield Road and Western Bank, and with a hill to contend with, it made electrical operation hazardous – hence the employment of a pointsman. From the following day the points would be permanently set for cars to turn left only for Crookes. A close look at the second pole from the right shows a new coil of wire hanging ready for the following day's realignment of the overhead.

The overhanging canopy of the old Scala Cinema can quite clearly be seen on the right on the corner of Brook Street. Opened on 23 December 1921, it had the additional facility of a ballroom on the second floor, a cafe on the first floor and an assembly room in the basement used for whist drives. It closed as a cinema on 5 July 1952 and was subsequently occupied by the University Department of Biochemistry before finally being demolished in 1964. Today this scene is virtually unrecognisable, with a large increase in the volume of vehicular traffic. *R. J. Wiseman*

Here is another scene that has all but vanished, as Rocker panel car No 383 picks up a passenger carrying a wooden basket of Guernsey tomatoes and a galvanised bucket. It is a Friday afternoon, 24 June 1955, and represents a scene that, at the time, would have seemed one of permanence. However, wholesale demolition would take place over the ensuing years with the Post Office in the right background being one of the first casualties. The bespectacled gentleman on the right (does anyone recognise him?) looks askance at the photographer, while mother and brood head homewards after popping into the 'Ices & Drinks' shop on Weston Place. *R. J. Wiseman*

Above On a quiet Saturday afternoon in Mowbray Street at its junction with Harvest Lane, domed-roof Standard car No 239 ambles along en route to Woodseats.

A large billboard advertising Guinness brightens an otherwise fairly drab scene. At this time the advertising agency that was employed by Guinness came up with some extremely clever and well-remembered creations. The one shown here has a pair of toucans sat in a tree guarding pints of 'Liffey Water' with the wording: 'Toucans in their nests agree, Guinness is good for you, Open some today and see, What one or Toucan do'. Pure genius! *R. J. Wiseman*

Below A delivery bicycle is the only other road vehicle in sight apart from the three trams working the intensive service from Woodseats to Wadsley Bridge. On a bright sunny Saturday 1 June 1957, car 297 heads along Mowbray Street towards Wadsley Bridge, while No 74 makes its way to Woodseats passing an advert issued by the Fish Federation to try and encourage the population to eat fish on other than a Friday! *R. J. Wiseman*

Where else could this be but the Neepsend Tavern (now the Fairfield Inn) with accompanying gasometers at Hillfoot Bridge? On the same day as the previous photograph Standard car No 83 and Roberts car No 536 turn in and out of Neepsend Lane respectively on their way to Woodseats and Wadsley Bridge. The public house survives today (although no longer Tetleys), as do the gasholders, unlike both trams, which ended their days in Ward's scrapyard at Tinsley. In 1952 No 536 was the last tram to be built for Sheffield, being one of 36 similar 'Jubilee' or 'Roberts' cars. It was, coincidentally, also the last car to move from Tinsley depot across the road to Ward's to meet its ultimate fate – see page 126. *R. J. Wiseman*

This view of Neepsend Lane on a fine, sunny 1 June 1957 shows the narrow confines of the thoroughfare with three domed-roof Standard cars, including Nos 267 and 269, negotiating one of the two stretches of single-track operation on this route. Control of the single-line sections was by means of colour lights operated by a mechanism in the overhead – 267's trolley is about to pass under an example. Despite the additional hazards of single-line working, the service from Woodseats to Wadsley Bridge via Neepsend lasted until Saturday 3 October 1959. *R. J. Wiseman*

On the same day as the previous photograph, 1 June 1957, Roberts car No 509 sets off along Neepsend Lane after taking on board a passenger at Boyland Street outside the Hallamshire Steel & File Co Ltd, with its 'Man of Steel' emblem just underneath 509's trolley head. *R. J. Wiseman*

Finally in this trio of views in Neepsend Lane on 1 June 1957, Standard car No 229 swings round the bend and passes Rutland Road with what appears to have been a former public house on the corner, today the site of the modern William Stones Cannon Brewery. The gable-end advert for Stones Ales reminds the author of the potency of this brew some long time ago in the Moulders Rest outside Rotherham Masborough station. Enough said! *R. J. Wiseman*

Above At the historic location of Bridgehouses Goods Station, domed-roof Standard car No 239 stops to pick up passengers at the junction of Nursery Street and Chatham Street on her way to Woodseats on Saturday 1 June 1957. On the site of the goods yard stood the location of the first railway from Manchester, dating back to 1845. The British Railways van to the left of the station sign is advertising five-day Sheffield Seaside Express tickets for 57s 6d, while the hoardings proclaim the benefits of Mackeson stout, Colman's lump starch, Players, and the recently revived Spangles – sweets that I am sure most of us had forgotten about. *R. J. Wiseman*

Below This almost deserted scene on Nursery Street was also photographed on Saturday 1 June 1957 – almost

unbelievable compared with the vast amount of traffic that thunders past this spot today. However, here we see domed-roof Standard car No 119 about to leave the first stretch of single track that was to be found on this part of the system, the other being that already encountered a little further along on Neepsend Lane. The traffic light control that regulated tramway traffic along these single stretches can be clearly seen on the pole on the right-hand side.

The blackened outline of Holy Trinity church is clearly visible in the centre of the picture. Consecrated on 13 October 1848, it had a seating capacity of 840. It was damaged in the Great Flood of 1864 when waters reached the tops of the pews. It remains today, albeit minus its pinnacles and balustrades, and now rejoices under the name of the New Testament Church of God Inc.

John Aizlewood's Crown Flour Mills building (or at least part of it) can also be clearly seen. The mill was originally built in 1861 on the site of the former Nursery Gardens of Sheffield Castle and alongside Sheffield's first railway – the Manchester, Sheffield & Lincolnshire – which carried grain from the cornfields of the latter county. The business continued under the auspices of the Aizlewood family until 1962 when it was sold to Associated British Foods. Closed as a flour mill in 1969, it became a farmers' merchants until it finally closed in 1984. The building subsequently became derelict and was left to the ravages of the weather and vandals until it was ultimately transformed into the Aizlewood Business Centre and stands today as a monument to foresight and planning and a triumph of conservation over destruction. *R. J. Wiseman*

THE OUTER SUBURBS

Above We start our tour of the outer suburbs at Pitsmoor, in the north of the city, with a real period piece. Rocker panel car No 411, looking decidedly travel weary though sporting a new set of indicator blinds, is about to reverse at Pitsmoor and make her way back to Meadowhead. It is Sunday 4 October 1953 and all is fairly quiet as the car is about to pick up the waiting passengers, some no doubt bound for hospital visits.

A splendid array of shops, erected in 1905, forms the background. Unlike today, Sunday opening did not exist and Andrew's the drapers, The Firth Park Creamery, Oliver's the greengrocers and Bill Beevers' motorcycle shop quietly observe the Sabbath. All the property is still standing today, although most have changed ownership. Bill Beevers' shop opened within weeks of the war ending in 1945, initially concentrating on the retailing of cameras and photographic equipment, mainly through the lack of availability of new motorbikes. The business continues to thrive today. *R. J. Wiseman*

Above right The clock in Olive Field's hairdressers window tells us that it is 5.20pm on a warm summer day,

1 July 1957. Olive is offering modern styling and cutting with cold waving – sounds painful! A period invalid carriage is parked outside. Two Standard cars, Nos 119 and 191, together with Roberts car No 526, are seen here at Pitsmoor junction. The driver of No 191 bears a striking resemblance to Mr McKay, the Chief Prison Officer of TV's Slade Prison – surely not! *R. J. Wiseman*

Further up Firth Park Road is this familiar location at Bellhouse Road where both rails and roundabout still exist today, although sadly the roundabout is in a much sorrier state. If it is intended to retain it, perhaps the Parks Department could be persuaded to make it more attractive and maybe uncover the tramlines once more as a reminder of former times. Domed-roof Standard car No 259 passes through the island on her way to Woodseats in May 1958 in an otherwise little-changed scene. *R. J. Wiseman*

Above The glorious, long summer of 1959 is still much in evidence here in September as a lady, off to the shops complete with wicker basket, crosses by the zebra as Roberts car No 507 heads through the Bellhouse Road roundabout on its way to Sheffield Lane Top. The Rev D. H. Jefferson and Councillor P. Robinson are to be the preachers on the following Sunday at Firth Park Methodist Church, built in 1911 and surviving to this day. Its somewhat blackened appearances is 'relieved' to some extent by generations of pigeon droppings! *John Fozard collection*

Below A queue of five trams headed by Roberts car No 516 has been held up waiting for sister car 513 to use the crossover at Firth Park and return to Woodseats on 22 July 1957. No 513 was one of the two survivors of the class; both it and No 510 were specially painted for the final week of operation and took part in the farewell procession.

No 510 was to be ultimately taken to the National Tramway Museum at Crich, Derbyshire, where she has remained ever since, whereas 513 has had a more eventful life since withdrawal from the Sheffield system. It spent several years in a variety of locations before finally finding a home at the Open Air Museum at Beamish, where it still carries passengers on a regular basis. However, in 1985 it made a trip to the seaside and visited Blackpool to run on the promenade to celebrate the town's tramway centenary, returning to Beamish the following year.

Note the small boy on the right complete with scooter. Children's outdoor pursuits and games were still very much part of the street scene in 1957 – the dreaded computer and its attendant (infuriating!) games were still a long way off. The Methodist Church still stands today, as do the row of shops with perhaps a lick of brighter paint on the buildings and the inevitable increase in vehicular traffic. *R. J. Wiseman*

It is clearly autumn in the positively sylvan setting of Stubbin Lane corner at its junction with Barnsley Road, as fully lined-out Rocker panel car No 500 leans into the steeply angled curve on a quiet Sunday 4 October 1953. No 500 has just left Lane Top and is making her way to Exchange Street in the City via Attercliffe. The extension from Bellhouse Lane up to Lane Top opened in 1934 and would see its last tram on 2 April 1960. *R. J. Wiseman*

Above The unmistakable location of Sheffield Lane Top terminus is seen here on 18 May 1957 with Standard car No 212 and wartime rebuild car No 483. One of the many branches of the Brightside & Carbrook Co-op can be clearly seen on the left, while the Prospect Hotel is sandwiched between the two trams. The last tram from here, wartime rebuild car No 100, ran on 2 April 1960. *R. J. Wiseman*

Below Returning to Pitsmoor junction, we now take the route towards Brightside along Page Hall Road and Upwell Street. On the pleasant sunny evening of Thursday

27 June 1957 domed-roof Standard car No 262, built in 1937, has just left Firth Park Road and is heading off down Page Hall Road for Brightside.

Easiephit was a well-known chain of shoe shops at this time. On the far side of Firth Park Road, McGreggor's Cafe seems to be doing little business, while a Standard Vanguard and Ford Consul complete the scene. Trams last ran along Page Hall Road on Saturday 28 April 1959 when the service from Fitzalan Square to Sheffield Lane Top via Savile Street was abandoned. The scene is little changed today, although the Easiephit shop later became a betting-shop and McGreggor's a halal butcher! *R. J. Wiseman*

Above Builder Ralph Hill is busy with renovations at the Firth Park Hotel on Page Hall Road as Standard car No 74 is seen, also on 27 June 1957, with the shadows lengthening as it picks up and offloads passengers on its way to Sheffield Lane Top. Old Albion Ales became part of the Whitbread empire in later years. The hotel still stands today as a focal point in an area that, comparatively speaking, has seen little change. *R. J. Wiseman*

Below On the same day, at the junction of Upwell Street and Carlisle Street East, Standard cars 223 and 109 pass British Railways' Upwell Street Wharf on their respective ways to Sheffield Lane Top and City, Exchange Street. Four small boys, three of them in short trousers, run across the street paying the trams no heed – at that time they were just an ordinary part of life. That was a time when smoking was also just an accepted way of life; the shops on the left are advertising no fewer than six different brands of cigarettes – Park Drive, Senior Service, Capstan, Players, Robin and Turf (whatever happened to them?) together St Bruno and Ogden tobacco. *R. J. Wiseman*

Above On the same evening Standard car No 223 is seen at Upwell Street and Owler Lane. The indicator blinds are all but unreadable, but probably say Sheffield Lane Top via Attercliffe. The property on the left looks to be extremely old and has been long demolished. Trams ceased running along Upwell Street in March 1958. *R. J. Wiseman*

Below Here is Upwell Street at the junction of Wensley Street a few days later on a warm 1 July 1957. The tram driver, in his full uniform, is also sporting a pair of sunglasses as the Ford van with typical impatient driver attempts to overtake on the offside. How many accidents and near-misses occurred over the years is impossible to judge. The inexorable advancement of the motor car and the inability of trams to 'get out of the way' gave the anti-tram lobby much-needed evidence to hasten their ultimate departure from virtually all the roads of towns and cities in the United Kingdom. *R. J. Wiseman*

On Wednesday afternoon, 8 May 1957, we see a busy scene on Attercliffe Common with a seemingly endless array of shops, many with their canvas sun blinds down (how much better than some of the gaudy plastic variety we see today). On the extreme left a squaddie (hands in pockets, tut tut!) passes by Althams, which seems to be a real 'open all hours' shop selling everything from mop buckets and stepladders to tins of lobster at 4 shillings! The whitewash writing on shop windows was once such a familiar sight – small boys passing by often erased some of the letters, making the advertised product take on a whole new meaning!

Standard car No 246 turns into Newhall Road on her way to Sheffield Lane Top past the multitude of Victorian streets that made up the thriving community of Attercliffe, which is much changed today following widespread demolition of older property, while the road is now horrendously busy! *R. J. Wiseman*

Here is perhaps the archetypal Sheffield industrial scene, with housing and adjacent steelworks combining to produce a Lowry-esque landscape – only the tall chimneys are missing. It is Saturday 23 April 1960 as Roberts car No 536 prepares to leave Weedon Street, Tinsley, and return to Leopold Street in the city centre. No 536 was the last car of the class to be delivered and entered service on 11 April 1952, thus seeing only a mere eight years on the road. The car stands out well against the smoke-blackened buildings and reflects the first-class order in which the Transport Department kept not only the fleet of trams but also the whole system infrastructure.

The scene here is animated by two small girls dashing across the street to join their friends, the man atop the three-section extension ladder on the left (rather him than me!), with his handcart positioned outside the front gate of the house at which he is working, and the little girl eyeing the cameraman curiously. A fine example of a pre-war Ford complements the scene. *Steve Palmer*

Routes to Darnall, Handsworth and Intake turned right off Attercliffe Road to travel down Staniforth Road. Here are two views of bridge-widening work on Staniforth Road in 1956. The canal bridge further down the road had been widened some years earlier and now it was the turn of the railway bridge, also known as the 'iron bridge'. In the first view domed roof car No 295, with trolley swinging wide, crosses the workings complete with pipework, compressor and Sheffield Corporation City Engineers crane on 28 March. *R. J. Wiseman*

The second view of the works was taken some three months later, on 23 June, looking the other way, and shows Standard car No 107 making her way to Darnall and Elm Tree, Intake. The cyclists did not have much room to manoeuvre when the trams swung almost to the kerbside. Note the lady with the wicker shopping basket. When the work was eventually completed, a double tram track was laid (having previously been interlaced), but this would last for a mere two more years until abandonment of the service to Elm Tree. *A. K. Terry*

Above left On a dull Friday afternoon on 3 May 1957 on Staniforth Road outside the Regal Cinema, a crowd of about 20 people wait to board Standard car No 110 bound for Darnall and Elm Tree, Intake, via Prince of Wales Road. There seems to be a sprinkling of school children complete with leather satchels and a small boy in shorts and wearing boots. Two Standard Vanguards head towards the camera.

The Regal, which was built on the site of the Theatre Royal, was opened on 14 October 1935 and closed on 27 May 1961. It became the inevitable bingo hall before being finally demolished. The film *Red Ball Express* was the main feature at this date; made in 1952, it starred Jeff Chandler, Sidney Poitier, Hugh O'Brien and Jack Kelly, and was described as 'a standard US war adventure, not too convincingly mounted but providing the usual excitements'. *R. J. Wiseman*

Left Most photographs in this book were taken in fine weather, but this shot serves to prove that it did actually rain in Sheffield in the 1950s! It was taken after a heavy downpour, although even here the sunshine is just starting to break through the gloom. Roberts car No 510 is pictured turning into Prince of Wales Road at Darnall junction on 4 October 1956 on her way to Intake; the through service to Intake via Elm Tree would cease two days later, although trams would continue straight on from this spot to Handsworth until 4 May 1957.

No 510 was one of 35 similar cars built for Sheffield Transport Department by Charles Roberts of Horbury, Wakefield. They entered service between 12 May 1950 and 11 April 1952, and were based on car 501, built at

Queens Road in 1946 exactly 50 years after the Corporation took over the Sheffield Tramways Company system in 1896; the class thus became known as either 'Jubilee' or 'Roberts' cars. What superbly designed trams they were with their graceful lines and curves – I don't think they would look out of place running on today's modern system.

On the left a wagon makes a beer delivery (in wooden barrels!) to the Rose and Crown, still at this spot today. *R. J. Wiseman*

Above The unused track and severed overhead of the Handsworth route can quite clearly be seen in this shot of the same junction taken on 10 March 1958; trams to Handsworth last ran on 4 May 1957. Roberts car No 502 entered service on 12 May 1950, being the first of the class proper, the precursor, No 501, having been constructed in 1946. No 502 is making her way up to Elm Tree, Intake, which, at the time of this photograph, had only a few weeks left to operate, the last car running on 12 April 1958. Buses, like the AEC Regal seen here on its way to Ballifield, were becoming more and more common as the trams gradually disappeared.

The Guinness advert is typical of the period, while at the Plaza, Handsworth, the film *No Down Payment* starring Joanne Woodward was the main 'X' certificate feature. The Plaza opened on 27 December 1937 and closed on 29 September 1963, becoming the home of bingo, then snooker. Rotherham United are at home to Barnsley, while Sheffield United reserves are due to play West Bromwich Albion reserves and Preston North End reserves in rapid succession. *A. K. Terry*

Above left On Saturday 18 April 1953 we see a remarkably quiet scene at the junction of Main Road and Prince of Wales Road. Trams to Handsworth are still running, and Standard car No 125 turns into Prince of Wales Road revealing a fine view of Darnall Cinema on Catliffe Road. First opened on 15 September 1914, it closed as a cinema on 2 November 1957 to become a furniture showroom.

The adverts on the left are also noteworthy, with *Lure of the Wilderness* and *Affair in Trinidad* showing at the Plaza, while Sheffield United are entertaining West Ham United on this day – the Blades won 2-1 in front of a crowd of 32,403, with Brook (2) and Browning the scorers. This was to be a good season for United, who ultimately completed their fixtures as Second Division Champions. *R. J. Wiseman*

Left Moving along the Handsworth route we see domed-roof Standard car No 270, built in 1937, pausing at Clifton Crescent, Handsworth Road, to offload passengers on the warm late afternoon of Monday 25 June 1956. 'Ediswan', as advertised on the side of the tram, was founded in 1881 as the Edison & Swan United Electric Light Company, a merger of Swan and Edison – formerly rival concerns. *R. J. Wiseman*

Above On Handsworth Road, outside the Parish Church of St Mary, Standard car 89 makes its way to Crookes on 28 April 1957. The church dates from the 12th century and is of mixed styles of architecture including transition, Norman and perpendicular. The tower and spire were rebuilt in 1825 and the body of the church was partly rebuilt in 1832. Stonemasons Lidster & Son were obviously very handily placed for the nearby graveyard! *A. K. Terry*

Turning right at Darnall junction, the Intake route followed Prince of Wales Road and passed beneath the former Great Central/LNER railway line. On a cold 18 April 1953 the early stages of the Manchester-Sheffield railway electrification via Woodhead Tunnel, completed the following year, can clearly be seen with the gantry on the right awaiting the rigging of the overhead wiring. An ex-Great Central Robinson 'O4' 2-8-0 freight locomotive rumbles along in the background hauling a huge string of laden, loose-coupled coal wagons – yet another image that has long disappeared. Roberts car 502 is setting down a passenger, while just behind the two ladies on the left-hand side is an example of the sewer gas evacuation lamps that were dotted around the city. These lamps, unlike the usual variety that went on and off by a clock mechanism, evacuated methane gases from the sewers and consequently were permanently lit. *R. J. Wiseman*

A closer view of Prince of Wales Road railway bridge on Monday 10 March 1958, with the remnants of a previous snowfall still in evidence. Domed-roof Standard car No 119 is nicely framed beneath the bridge as ex-LMS '8F' 2-8-0 locomotive No 48143 rumbles overhead with another rake of loose-coupled coal wagon empties – note that the electrification wiring is now in place. Some 849 of these locomotives were built, and they were considered highly successful workhorses. Some of the class lasted right until the end of steam operation in 1968 working from Rose Grove Motive Power Depot, Burnley. The 'lion and wheel' emblem on the engine's tender was the first symbol to represent the nationalised railway system, other than the wording 'British Railways', and was variously known as the 'Ferret and Dartboard' or 'Starved Lion'. How dramatically the railways have changed since the 1950s, with goods trains like this being so common, yet now completely a thing of the past. It is interesting to see how Prince of Wales Road narrowed at this spot. Today the railway bridge is painted in a brighter colour and has the maker's name, Hemingways of Middlesbrough, and the year of manufacture, 1900, highlighted.

The Brightside & Carbrook Co-op van advertises the fact that 'rubber soling and heeling wears twice as long', presumably compared with leather, and, no doubt, twice as cheap. In those days the Co-op, as in every other town and city, provided a service for almost anything. *A. K. Terry*

This striking panoramic view of Prince of Wales Road was taken from the top deck of a tram making the descent to Darnall. The forerunner of the class of 'Jubilee' or Roberts cars, No 501, begins the long climb up to Manor Top, Elm Tree. Today the ascent up Prince of Wales Road is interrupted by the modern Sheffield Parkway; although the tramway reservation remains, it has long since been grassed over. Who knows, one day it may be thought worthwhile to extend the Supertram system down to Darnall and link up at Meadowhall. *A. K. Terry*

A fine view of three trams on the triangular junction at Manor Top, Elm Tree. The late winter shadows of 27 March 1956 lengthen as 1933-built Standard car No 123 drops off a passenger before heading down Prince of Wales Road, while an unidentified domed-roof Standard is about to depart down Mansfield Road to Intake. Imagine dropping someone off at this point in the middle of the road today! During a 1994 visit to the city to take some present-day photographs for the original edition of this book, Manor Top was just getting back to some semblance of order after enduring great upheaval preparing for a new extension of the Supertram system, which was then about to open. *R. J. Wiseman*

Below A first-class three-quarter view of domed-roof Standard wartime rebuild car No 119 at rest at Manor Top, Elm Tree, at the top of Prince of Wales Road. What fine, sturdy cars these were, some of them providing faithful service right until the final abandonment; No 119 was withdrawn from service in October 1959. This particular shot was taken in May 1957 when the tramway at Manor Top was just a shadow of its former self. The triangular junction had long gone, with just the Prince of Wales Road cars terminating prior to reaching the new roundabout.

The Manor Cinema in the background opened on 12 December 1927 and closed to become a bingo hall on 21 July 1963. It finally closed on 14 June 1969 to be converted into a supermarket, which is still operating today. The main feature on this day in 1957 was *A Touch of the Sun*, which had a huge array of British stars including Frankie Howerd, Ruby Murray, Reginald Beckwith, Richard Wattis, Dennis Price and Alfie Bass. *John Fozard collection*

Bottom On a sunny day in May 1956 at Manor Top, Elm Tree, Standard car No 74, having traversed the length of Prince of Wales Road, turns into Mansfield Road and on to Birley Vale, Intake. The lines and overhead in the right foreground have been severed, the last trams to use City Road and Duke Street having made their final journeys from Intake to Walkley on 7 April 1956. However, the line leading from Prince of Wales Road to Intake, as seen here, lasted until October 1956 when a new roundabout was subsequently installed; services thereafter terminated at the top of Prince of Wales Road.

An AEC Regal bus climbs the hill and passes the Elm Tree Hotel, which is still there today in an area that, from a traffic point of view, has much changed, having seen a huge increase in volume. *R. J. Wiseman*

A very quiet, late Sunday afternoon, 20 September 1953, sees domed-roof car 288 heading for Intake down Mansfield Road at the junction of Woodhouse Road. Just two television aerials are visible in the whole scene in a year that saw the Coronation of Her Majesty Queen Elizabeth II and still probably the most exciting

FA Cup Final of all time – the Matthews final when Blackpool beat Bolton Wanderers 4-3. But then I'm biased! I think the picture has an air of utter timelessness about it. *R. J. Wiseman*

Standard car No 76, showing clearly the advantage of the trolley reverser, sets off on the cross-city journey to Walkley from Intake terminus at Birley Vale. It is Saturday 7 April 1956, the last day of operation of the direct route to Walkley, although trams would still continue running down to this point via Prince of Wales Road until October

1956. The extension from Woodhouse Road to Birley Vale was the final addition to the tramway system and was opened in two stages in 1935. A split-windscreen Morris Minor and, in the distance, a Ford Prefect, complete the scene. *A. K. Terry*

Continuing our clockwise tour of Sheffield's suburbs, we arrive at the Beauchief and Meadowhead routes. This is Abbeydale Road in the final year of tramway operation, 1960. The precursor of the domed-roof Standard class, No 231, is captured in the lengthening shadows as she makes her way to Vulcan Road past some splendid examples of quality suburban homes with their, by now, forests of TV aerials sprouting from almost every chimney stack. How ugly they looked!

Fortunately smaller aerials would eventually take their place, although today's satellite dishes are equally becoming a blot on the landscape.

No 231 was a real survivor. Having been built in 1936, she saw service until the very last day of operation, only to suffer the final ignominy of being eventually broken up at Thomas Ward's scrapyard. *R. J. Wiseman*

Above Millhouses turning circle was the only one on the system, seen here on Monday 23 May 1960. Domed-roof Standard car 286 is seen entering the circle complete with smiling driver, prior to returning to Angel Street in the city centre. The Waggon & Horses Hotel is shown to good advantage in the background with someone just having thrown a shovelful of coal on the bar fire. *Steve Palmer*

Below Moments later, an equally enthusiastic conductor waves from the platform. The fine parade of shops in the background includes Malone's the Chemist, F. Corker (not Porker!) the Butcher, M. A. Mizon's frock shop, the Harrington Fruit Stores and Millhouses Bakeries. In another few months this particular scene would be but a memory. Although the trams ran from Millhouses right until the very last day of operation, the turning circle was converted for bus use some weeks earlier. *Steve Palmer*

It is 1.55pm on 19 January 1955 and brilliant winter sunshine has followed recent snowfall. This truly superb shot shows Standard car No 197, having dropped off the gentleman with the wicker shopping basket, leaving the Millhouses tram stop and heading off down Abbeydale Road bound for Vulcan Road. Roberts car No 534, having used the turning circle, pauses before setting off for Weedon Street. The folding platform doors on these cars were something of a bonus for drivers in wintertime compared with the older cars with their open platforms. As Sheffield snowfalls go, this one seems to have been reasonably light, the roadway having been salted and cleared. *R. J. Wiseman*

Above Roberts cars 521 and 530 are seen at Millhouses tram terminus on 24 September 1960 with only a couple of weeks before the whole tram system would be no more. The turning circle, which had been part of the scene here for many years, had been converted into a bus turning circle by this time, and a trolley reverser was installed on 29 August 1960, which lasted for only six weeks. Its method of operation is clearly shown here, and avoided the conductor having to turn the trolley manually with a long pole, which is what happened on many other tramway undertakings in the United Kingdom. They were a most common sight in Sheffield and could be seen at almost every terminus and crossover, the first one having been installed as long ago as December 1915.

The AEC 'Fina' petrol tanker on the right would have been considered a large vehicle in 1960 but, by comparison with today's huge juggernauts, seems very moderate. *R. J. Wiseman*

Below A cold Wednesday 19 January 1955 provides a winter's scene at one of the tramway system's extremities, Beauchief. Standard car No 194 turns off the reserved track on Abbeydale Road South into Abbey Lane on its journey back to Firth Park via Pitsmoor. To the right of the upper deck of No 194 and the chimney stack on the building behind can be seen a contact in the overhead, which, when activated by the trolley, caused the traffic lights to turn to red for other road users, giving priority to the tram to cross the road. *R. J. Wiseman*

Above In another perfect winter's scene Rocker panel car No 489 drifts and sways gently down Abbey Lane en route for Vulcan Road on Sunday 7 February 1954. The road and reserved tram track have been cleared of snow and the tall trees, long since shorn of their leaves, stand out starkly against the bright winter sky. This length of track from Woodseats to Beauchief was opened on 25 April 1927 and provided an excellent, though for the most part under-used, service that was in the main segregated from road traffic. The last tram ran along here on Saturday 28 February 1959; it seems such a lack of foresight and waste of money for a well-designed routeway to close merely because cheap oil and the diesel bus were in the ascendancy. However, as we know things have now come full circle with the introduction of the Supertram. *R. J. Wiseman*

Below After a fairly heavy fall of snow on a cold and bleak St Valentine's Day 1956, the sky seems to suggest that more is on the way. It makes one shiver just to look at it! Standard car No 124 makes her way along a slushy Abbey Lane en route for Firth Park via Pitsmoor, having dropped off a lone passenger at Linden Avenue. Not many people have ventured out yet judging by the lack of footprints in the snow. Notice the comparison between today's modern and highly effective street lighting and that shown here, which is very poor and must have given off very little illumination. *R. J. Wiseman*

Above Towards the end of Abbey Lane was Woodseats terminus. On 31 October 1955 Rocker panel car No 42 reverses at Camping Lane in readiness for the journey back to Wadsley Bridge. These cars were known by some as 'banjos' due to the odd window arrangement around the driver's vestibule, which had curved glass protruding to encompass the handbrake. Car 42 was built in 1924 by the Brush Engineering Company of Loughborough and eventually held the distinction of being the oldest passenger-carrying vehicle in the fleet prior to its withdrawal in 1957. Even though this photograph was taken almost 50 years ago, it seems quite staggering that a main road and tram route was still lit by gas – a splendid example of a typical four-mantle-burner lamp is shown to advantage on the left. *R. J. Wiseman*

Below The road sign on the left really says it all – the steep climb up from Woodseats to Meadowhead is perfectly captured here on Friday 24 July 1959 as Standard car No 97 and wartime rebuild No 483 pass each other by the compulsory Board of Trade stop on the left, denoted by the three white bands on the pole. The last tram to leave Meadowhead ran on Saturday 2 April 1960. *Steve Palmer*

The service from Ecclesall to Middlewood was the first major route to close after the war and was the forerunner on an ever-increasing programme of abandonment over the next 6½ years. How ironic that 40 years later the new Supertram would run to Middlewood again. Had anyone predicted this happening in the 1950s they would have probably been burned at the stake as a heretic!
This photograph of Eccleshall Road, dated Sunday 20 September 1953, gives a

fine example of just how the city climbs steeply from its centre on three sides. Standard car No 207 grinds up the hill passing Huntingtower Road on her way to Banner Cross and the terminus at Ecclesall just prior to a spectacular downpour. The array of shops on the left very much reflect the time, as do the two television aerials – soon to become an all too familiar feature. *R. J. Wiseman*

Above On the same Sunday morning as the previous photograph, the pleasant surroundings add to the charm of this peaceful scene as Standard car No 247 makes her way uphill from Banner Cross to the terminus at Ecclesall; the extension from Banner Cross was opened in 1922. The closure of this service from Middlewood to Ecclesall prompted an angry public response with a petition of more than 11,000 signatures presented to the Council opposing the move. On this occasion the petition was totally ignored; indeed, the tram-scrapping programme was enhanced and speeded up. What a lack of foresight! This particular scene shows five motor cars that would indeed be collector's items today. They include a Humber Hawk, a Ford VS Pilot, a Sunbeam Talbot and a Vauxhall. *R. J. Wiseman*

Below That Sunday morning's shower has come and gone as Roberts car No 507 climbs Ecclesall Road. This photograph serves to show what a city of contrasts Sheffield was, ranging from the heavy industrial areas of the east to the more countrified areas of the west and south. An electric van belonging to Chatsworth Dairy pauses to make a delivery. *R. J. Wiseman*

In a veritable Christmas card scene, Standard car No 198 poses outside All Saints Church, Ecclesall, on Sunday 7 February 1954, with the driver peering out to ensure that he is a part of the picture. It is doubtful whether All Saints saw many worshippers on this day as the fall of snow seems to have been quite heavy – definitely a Sunday to be spent around a roaring coal fire with a good book! *R. J. Wiseman*

Cars from Crookes either worked through to Handsworth or part of the route to Midland station. Here 1929-built Standard car No 144 leaves Crookes Road to join Witham Road on 12 April 1957; it is interesting to note that nine years after railway nationalisation the indicator blind still shows 'LMS Station'. The driver glances to his right to ensure that the road is clear as his car passes by the Laichung Chinese Laundry, which has clearly seen better days. The properties on the left have since been demolished and replaced by modern development, while that on the right survives but with changes of ownership. The *Sheffield Telegraph* billboard outside the newsagents proclaims that the 'Miners reject pay offer'. I make no comment – history must judge for itself. *R. J. Wiseman*

The sharp curves at the junction of Crookes Road and Whitham Road are clearly visible in this view as domed-roof Standard car No 266, with flanges squealing, turns out of Whitham Road on 8 April 1957. Until 23 August 1936 trams continued on from Whitham Road into Fulwood Road bound for Fulwood itself, but this route was discontinued after the extension from Hunters Bar, Eccleshall Road, to Fulwood was opened. In this scene a Ford van and, I think, a Guy Arab double-deck bus pull up Nile Street in surroundings that have, comparatively speaking, not changed quite so drastically as other parts of the city. *A. K. Terry*

Some heavy repair and points replacement is going on at Crookes tram terminus at Heavygate Road on Monday 21 March 1955. This was the highest terminus on the system, being some 630 feet above sea level, and gave spectacular views over the city. 1929-built Standard car No 131 uses the trolley reverser and commences a short working back to Church Street in the city centre. The scene also shows two air compressors, a tar boiler and a watchman's hut. The red danger flags are held upright by being inserted in old bits of tram rail; this was, of course, long before the advent of the flashing yellow warning lights with which we are so familiar today. *R. J. Wiseman*

The Walkley route was steep, twisting and narrow. The 'S' bend in Barber Road is shown here to good effect; the tramlines almost touch the kerb in places and woe betide anyone whose vehicle was parked incorrectly on a bend as the tram's overhang could pack a fair old clout!

Standard car No 108 climbs the steep incline passing a row of shops with greengrocers, grocers and Post Office clearly shown. Lyons Tea and Cakes are on sale at F. M. Williams the grocer, while Cadbury's prominently announce a reduction in prices. *A. K. Terry*

In a scene so very typical of all tramway systems throughout the country, here we see the permanent way gang, complete with tar boiler, pausing to allow domed-roof Standard car No 261 to proceed down Barber Road on her way to Intake. Track on many of the steeper sections of the Sheffield system had to be replaced at fairly regular intervals due to the use of track brakes, etc, and to avoid corrugations of the rail. It is interesting to note that all the gang, except the young man on the right, are wearing the almost obligatory flat cap, while the foreman is easily identifiable by his trilby! It is mid-afternoon on Friday 4 May 1955 with the gang hoping to complete as much as possible of the job before, no doubt, enjoying the heady delights of a Friday night out. Note the shopkeeper at the confectioners eyeing the scene and wondering how much longer the pile of setts is to remain on the pavement outside his shop. Laying and relaying setts was quite an art in itself – much more difficult than the brick paving we see in shopping precincts today. *R. J. Wiseman*

• 98 •

The steepness of the Walkley route is again shown to great effect here as Roberts car No 502 pulls up Barber Road on 24 March 1956 passing Kaye Place on the left, where the butcher is advertising New Zealand shoulder mutton for 2 shillings a pound! No 502 is looking a little worn here despite being only six years old. The side bracket arms supporting the overhead wires could be seen at a variety of locations on the system. Just look at all the chimney pots – not a gas flue in sight! *A. K. Terry*

Above On Saturday morning, 24 March 1956, two ladies, one looking curiously at the photographer, ignore the notice to 'Please form queue other side' and wait on Barber Road for the next car to town. Two Standard cars, including No 111, pass the other way heading for Walkley terminus. It seems incredible today that trams ran in such narrow streets, preventing any parking at all (perhaps no bad thing). This was, no doubt, the reason for this route's early abandonment some 15 days later. An Austin Somerset and Austin Devon follow the trams without being able to overtake, while some severe pruning of the tree of the left seems to have come to a temporary halt. *A. K. Terry*

Opposite page One particular point of interest on the Walkley route was the Barber Road 'hump'. Here we see two views of this remarkable location with its compulsory Board of Trade stop, denoted by the three white bands on the pole. Eight-wheeled cars would have never have made it over the top – trams seemed to literally balance precariously on the summit before moving off towards the terminus or the city. In the first view Standard car No 76 off-loads on the crest of the summit on 24 March 1956.

The Midland Bank building on the corner of Commonside in the second photograph still stands today, though not now used for banking purposes, and all the setts in the roadway have long been replaced. Domed-roof car No 241 was photographed on 24 June 1955. *A. K. Terry/R. J. Wiseman*

Above Domed-roof Standard car No 238 has just left Walkley terminus at South Road and heads for Intake on a cold, misty 24 March 1956. Notice how close the tram lines are to the kerbside, which, apart from the wider part outside the cinema on the right, gave the trams a free run as no other vehicle could even think about parking.

The Palladium Cinema opened on 17 December 1916 and closed on 6 October 1962. It was subsequently demolished, a supermarket eventually replacing it. On this particular day one of the films showing is *A Case for PC49* with Brian Reece in the starring role. A Hammer film made in 1950, it was, perhaps a little unfairly, described as 'an incompetent and virtually unwatchable transcription of a juvenile radio series'. From the author's memory, PC49 was a hugely popular wireless series from the late 1940s and early 1950s. The Guinness advert and splendid Jaguar car are also noteworthy items in this scene. *A. K. Terry*

Above right Parkside Road, Hillsborough, on the Middlewood route, was where trams on Football Specials 'laid over' until the game at the nearby stadium finished. It is a cold Saturday 20 March 1954 with a fine array of different types of car shown, including experimental car No 367. The latter provides a fine example of the elaborate lining used on the trams at this time, adverts having still not been applied to all vehicles. A cheery crew and brace of Inspectors, one with a points lever in his hand, pose for the camera.

Sheffield Wednesday are playing Arsenal and will win 2-1 in front of a crowd of 42,072, with Gannon and Sewell the scorers. The following Saturday the team, who were having a good FA Cup run, were to play Preston North End in the semi-final at Maine Road, Manchester, in front of a crowd of 75,213! Unfortunately they lost 2-0, which must have knocked the stuffing out of them as they were to win only one more game that season and finish 19th in Division 1 of the Football League. Older readers will recall some famous names playing at this time, including Sewell, Froggatt, Woodhead, Shaw, Finney and Quixall. *R. J. Wiseman*

Right Another view of Parkside Road shows the truncated tracks that led into Middlewood Road; services along here from Middlewood to Ecclesall ceased on 28 March 1954. The floodlights of Wednesday's ground can quite clearly be seen. Here on Saturday 12 April 1958 we see three of the stacked cars, including Standard No 62 and Roberts car No 510 posing in the sunshine. Wednesday were at home to Everton, and recorded one of the few wins that season – 2-1 was the final score, with Quixall and Curtis ensuring victory in front of, for them, a miserable crowd of only 18,715. The 1957-58 season was a particularly bad one for the club, and saw them finishing in bottom place and being relegated to Division 2. It would also be the last full season for the legendary Albert Quixall's playing days with Wednesday. He was subsequently transferred to Manchester United, becoming then the most expensive footballer in Britain, United having paid what today is a paltry sum, a mere £45,000! *A. K. Terry*

On a really filthy day like this, melting snow makes life miserable for everyone. It is Sunday 7 February 1954 on Middlewood Road, again at the junction of Parkside Road. Standard cars Nos 192 and 199 pause to disgorge passengers while journeying to Ecclesall and Middlewood respectively. Only a few more weeks of the service would remain before abandonment on 28 March 1954. No 199 would ultimately become the last car to run in the old livery of Prussian blue and cream, while No 192 was a wartime rebuild of a car destroyed in the Blitz of 1940. *R. J. Wiseman*

Two schoolgirls pass by the cyclist who is struggling up Halifax Road and keeping his distance from approaching domed-roof car No 296, which is also tackling the steeply graded road on its way to Wadsley Bridge. It is a dull 8 July 1957 with, perhaps, the only thing to brighten the day being the thoughts of a holiday in Cleethorpes and a visit to Wonderland, 'England's largest Covered-in Amusement Park', where reduced prices for organised parties were an added inducement. The Wadsley Bridge to Woodseats route was abandoned on Saturday 3 October 1959. *A. K. Terry*

PRESERVED CARS

Above left Roberts car No 510 poses in Queens Road on Sunday 2 October 1960 during a tour, undertaken together with sister cars 513 and 501, of the remaining system. As can clearly be seen, the car had been specially painted for the last week of operation depicting various different types of tram that had run over the years right back to horse car operation in 1873. Car 513 was also similarly painted but with detail differences. No 510 was subsequently preserved and has resided at the National Tramway Museum at Crich, Derbyshire, since moving there in October 1960. *John Fozard collection*

Left Like sister car 510, No 513 was specially repainted for the last week of operation and ran in the final procession. It too survived breaking up, but unlike 510 has had a more chequered and sometimes exciting career since. In 1985 it visited Blackpool as part of the town's tramway centenary celebrations and looked very much at home alongside the Blackpool English Electric double-deck streamline cars.

No 513 is seen here at the junction of Upwell Street and Wensley Street on 1 July 1957 bound for Sheffield Lane Top. What looks to be a tram driver and his conductress off duty overtake on their motorbike, before the advent of compulsory crash helmets. The newsagent and tobacconist on the left is very reminiscent of the era with its multiplicity of adverts outside, including one for the comic *Film Fun*. How many readers remember it and its sister comic *Radio Fun*? In the distance, to the left of the advert for Wall's Ice Cream, is a school road sign showing the 'flame of learning' – another part of the street scene that disappeared many years ago. *R. J. Wiseman*

Above Standard car No 189 undertook a Light Railway Transport League tour of the system on 30 March 1958, which resulted in a journey of almost 50 miles! Here we see the well-filled 189 at Wadsley Bridge terminus. The tram driver on this occasion was undertaking his last day of duty before transferring to buses. *A. K. Terry*

In a second picture taken during the LRTL tour, No 189 is nicely framed under Upwell Street bridge, complete with gas lamps; the road underneath the bridge was lowered in April 1922 to accommodate double-deck cars. Car 189 saw four more days in public service before being withdrawn and stored in Tinsley depot to re-emerge to take part in the final procession, having been purchased by the LRTL. She was ultimately removed to Crich where she was remained ever since. *A. K. Terry*

Domed-roof Standard car No 264 crosses Midland station junction on 4 May 1957. Although not planned at this time, 264 was to survive until the last day of tramway operation, and was then preserved to be transferred to Crich where she is to be found today. *R. J. Wiseman*

Works car No 330 was photographed outside Tenter Street depot on 23 May 1954. This was one of several cars from other cities purchased by the Transport Department during the Second World War to maintain and enhance services needed to cater for exceptional traffic resulting from round-the-clock industrial production and depleted bus services. Originally a double-deck car (see page 16), she lost her top deck when withdrawn from public service after the war to take up duties with the works fleet. She survived right until the end of tramway operation and is now also preserved at Crich.

Two boys swing on a gas lamp on the left (how those lamps provided hours of fun for children swinging with a rope from the bracket arm!), while a small girl pushes an upturned table on an old pram chassis. *R. J. Wiseman*

Depots, specials and incidents

Outside Tinsley depot we see a real parade of veterans on 1 May 1955. Tinsley was the original Sheffield Tramways Company depot and its engraved name above the entrance arches can still be seen to this day. Preston-built car 346 on the left is about to commence a special tour of the system, but pauses long enough to pose with sister cars 342 and 339, together with Rocker panel car 474. All four cars would have been withdrawn from service before the closure of the next route, that from Walkley to Intake on 7 April 1956. *A. K. Terry*

In this really excellent view, we see Roberts car No 516 at rest outside Tinsley depot on Friday 24 July 1959. What fine vehicles these Roberts cars were, with their two 65hp motors and upholstered seating for 62. They would not be out of place if they ran on the streets today.

Bassett's, as advertised on the side panel, are, of course, a part of Sheffield's history in their own right. Founded in 1842 by George Bassett, a general confectioner, the Sheffield connection goes back to 1858 with the setting up of a factory in Portland Street. In 1851 an apprentice, J. M. Thompson, joined the company and became a partner in about 1863. The Thompson family were to have a long connection with Basset's until 1974. One of the firm's most famous sweets are, of course, Liquorice Allsorts, first 'discovered' in 1899 purely by accident. The then sole salesman, Charlie Thompson, was discussing business with a customer when he knocked over his tray of samples, scattering the colourful sweets on the counter. The buyer liked the look of the mixed-up confectionery, placed an order, and Bassett's Liquorice Allsorts were born. Bassett's Jelly Babies are almost as famous; launched at the end of the First World War, they were originally called 'Peace Babies'. Production was halted during the Second World War but resumed in 1953, when they became known as Jelly Babies.

The famous logo of 'Bertie Bassett' goes back to 1929, and was loosely based on a similar logo for Michelin Tyres; both have stood the test of time remarkably well. Sweet production moved to the current premises in Livesey Street in 1941. Many takeovers of other companies, including Wilkinson's and Barratt's, have taken place over the years until, in March 1990, Bassett's themselves became known as Trebor-Bassett, a wholly owned subsidiary company of Cadbury Schweppes. *Steve Palmer*

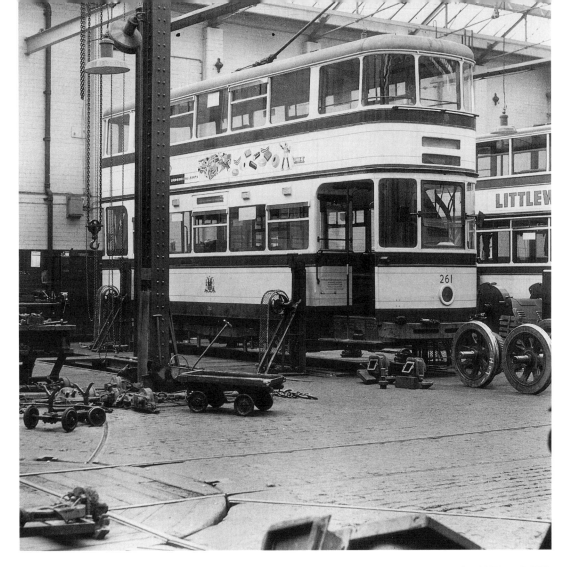

These two views were taken inside Queens Road Works on 17 June 1956. Wartime replacement car No 261, built in 1943, and Standard car No 163 are both 'sans wheels' and resting on jacks. New tyres are being fitted and the wheels in front of car 263 still bear the chalked word 'hot'. Those in front of No 163 clearly show the new tyre having been 'heated' on to the wheel.

The clock shows that it is 3.23pm, and there is not a workman in sight – hardly surprising, as it's a Sunday! All the paraphernalia of a tramcar works can be clearly seen, including axle turntable, trolleys, axleboxes, chain hoists, life-guard trays, lathes and vices. Queens Road works was opened in 1905 and a large percentage of the city's trams were built here over the years. *Both A. K. Terry*

Above This superb shot shows Roberts car No 503 posing outside Crookes depot on 13 August 1950. The car is in pristine condition, having only entered service a few weeks earlier. Thoroughly modern in every way, the Roberts cars were a great credit to their designers and were a fine example of just how tramway systems all over the United Kingdom should have kept up with the times and modernised their systems, as on the continent. What a great pity that car 503 and 34 of her sisters saw such a short period of service on the streets, only eight years in some cases, although 501, the forerunner of the class, had been built in 1946. Notice that the pole-painters have been busy outside the depot. *John Fozard collection*

Above right Inside Crookes depot on 28 April 1957 the inspection pits and overhead cleaners' galleries are clearly shown. Two of the cars pictured, Standards 199 and 210, had modest claims to fame: 199 was the last car to travel up Abbey Lane from Beauchief to Woodseats on 1 March 1959 and was also the last car to run in the old livery of Prussian blue and cream, while 210 was the last car to leave Wadsley Bridge on 3 October 1959.

The reason for many cars never receiving a new livery was said to be due to the 20 coats of paint each car was supposed to have been given (plus varnish), and the excellent quality of the pigments. *A. K. Terry*

Right This fairly rare shot taken inside Holme Lane depot on 20 March 1954 shows Preston-built car No 343 at rest with an unidentified domed-roof Standard car about to take up duty on the Middlewood-Ecclesall route. This route was abandoned seven days later and the depot itself would close on St George's Day, 23 April 1954. The route's closure enabled several older cars in the fleet to be withdrawn and broken up. The depot building survives to this day. *R. J. Wiseman*

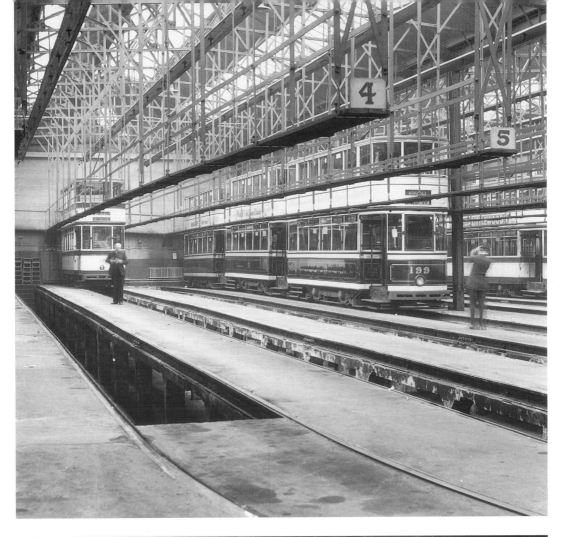

The vast bulk of St Luke's Church dominates the skyline above Midland station on a warm Sunday 13 August 1950 as Roberts car No 503, seen on the previous page, together with sister car 502 not shown here, undertakes a special tour of the tramway system. Both are virtually brand new, having only just entered service a week or so earlier.

The Sheffield City Transport wartime utility double-deck buses make an interesting comparison with the similar scene on page 35. The Cosy Café was around for many years, but the background beyond the railway has changed dramatically over the ensuing period to make way for the modern development of the Park Hill and Hyde Park flats, which were themselves to dominate the city skyline for many years. St Luke's Church was an early casualty of redevelopment. Designed by Flockton and Gibbs, it was consecrated on 30 September 1878. Its full title was actually St Luke's (Sale Memorial) Church and was so named after a previous vicar of Sheffield. It seated 640 people and was demolished in 1952. *John Fozard collection*

Above Four years later, on 30 October 1954, it's University Rag Day. Preston-built car No 346 has been suitably decorated by the Sheffield College of Art in the guise of a 'showboat' and is in Abbey Lane touring the system complete with an assortment of equally strangely attired students. The car was in public service, and no doubt intending passengers had to cough up more than their fare when boarding – I suspect many waited for the next one to come along! *R. J. Wiseman*

Right The following year, on Sunday 1 May 1955, 1907-built No 346 is pictured at Meadowhead terminus on the occasion of a Light Railway Transport League tour of the system, which, at this time, was still substantial. The five-hour trip took in almost every part of the many routes still operating. The only portion not being attempted was from Manor Top down City Road and Duke Street, as this type of car, which did not have air brakes, was barred from operating on those thoroughfares. *A. K. Terry*

Although published before, this shot, taken in the early hours of 8 April 1956, is so good that I feel it is worthy of inclusion; I suspect that many people will not have seen it before in any case. Standard car No 94 and Roberts car No 505 are at Manor Top; despite the latter's indicator saying 'Intake', it has just come up from there and is about to descend City Road and Duke Street as the last car ever to do so, or so it was thought! Although considered slightly eccentric at the time, it is fortunate that such enthusiastic people as photographers existed, otherwise much of what is recorded in this book, and countless other publications like it, would be but a memory. *A. K. Terry*

A couple of weeks later, Sunday 29 April 1956 saw a tour of epic proportions organised by the Light Railway Transport League. Rocker panel car No 42 and Standard car No 1, the last car to be built by Cravens of Darnall in 1927, were used. Here No 1 uses the Chippinghouse Road crossover in Abbeydale Road; this crossover was mainly used by football specials to Sheffield United's ground, which, after reversing, moved on to Wolseley Road to await the game's final whistle. The Hillman van would now be something of a period piece, while one of the three girls on the left enjoys the almost forgotten art of skipping as they head towards the paper shop for some sweets. *R. J. Wiseman*

Above This unmistakeable location is Crookes terminus, with No 1 in residence during the LRTL tour seen on the previous page. Passengers prepare to re-embark after taking photographs while an Inspector chats to the crew of domed-roof Standard car No 266, which has parked at the absolute last inch of track available before it would collide with the bollard in the centre of the track. *A. K. Terry*

Below No 1 – showing a highly contrived indicator blind! – is at rest in Cherry Street, which was used for football specials to Sheffield United's home games. The adverts on the hoarding are much as today, particularly the lurid details of the nun who was lured away from the Convent to experience life in the bright lights! This was appearing in the current issue of *The People* – as we say, some things never change! No 1 was to survive for a further year in service and was withdrawn after closure of the Crookes-Handsworth route on 4 May 1957. *A. K. Terry*

Above Just a year later, on Sunday 28 April 1957, Nos 42, 52 and 497, the last three Rocker panel cars in service, took part in another Light Railway Transport League tour, and the trio are pictured at the tour's commencement on the single track in Angel Street. After the abandonment of the Middlewood-Ecclesall route on 28 March 1954, the track lost its double status and was mainly used for access to Tenter Street depot. Angel Street suffered badly during the air raids of December 1940 and only limited rebuilding has taken place. The 'new' Brightside & Carbrook Co-operative Society on the right was, due to post-war building restrictions, still only single-storey. *R. J. Wiseman*

Below Two of the cars on the same tour are seen later in the afternoon about to enter Paternoster Row and make their way up to Moorhead. *John Fozard collection*

A pleasant sunny day in Waingate on 1 June 1957 sees three Standard cars in different guises: No 217 is on its way up to Pitsmoor in the new livery, 63 is bound for Sheffield Lane Top, showing the normal large numerals associated with the old livery, while 71 is on a special tour. This latter car was unique in having the more modern Gill Sans numerals on both ends. The Jubilee advert on the right extols the virtues of a very popular stout brewed at the Hope & Anchor Brewery in Sheffield. *R. J. Wiseman*

Domed-roof Standard car No 283 crosses the junction of West Bar Green on the fine Saturday afternoon of 12 April 1958 on a tour of the system. The Surrey Hotel on the left has seen much better days and now lies derelict. Further down West Bar is the paint shop of J. L. Dobb & Son Ltd, which some readers may recall. *A. K. Terry*

In March 1960 Standard car No 222 and Roberts car No 502 are on a special tour, ascending High Street to wander off round what was left of the system. No 222 eventually held the distinction of being the very last car in public service when she ran from Beauchief to Tinsley depot on the final day of operation, 8 October 1960.
John Fozard collection

Like any other large tramway undertaking, Sheffield had its share of tramcar breakdowns, overhead wires coming adrift for one reason or another, accidents and, as shown here, trolleys rendering themselves useless, usually as a result of de-wiring. On 8 July 1957 we see Standard car No 237 thus disabled and being pushed clear of the junction with Staniforth Road and Attercliffe Road by sister car No 222, seen opposite. Presumably the disabled car will be pushed to Tinsley depot to await repair.

The Sheffield Savings Bank on the left ultimately became part of the TSB but closed in 1989, its business transferring to the new Meadowhall complex. Who exactly 'The Rope Man' was on the Bedford lorry following the incident is unknown, but I am sure some readers will have the answer. Note the Vauxhall Velox on the left with its white-walled tyres – the American influence was still very prevalent in 1957. *A. K. Terry*

Above left The clock on the lamp post says 3.29pm on the final day of tramway operation, 8 October 1960. From lunchtime the weather had worsened and the heavens opened to add to the general depressive air of the day. Here we see Roberts car No 515, looking in a decidedly weary state, coming out of service and entering Tinsley depot for the last time. It would only have one more short journey to make – just across the road to Thomas Ward's for breaking up.

The rain did not let up and the final procession later on was held in appalling conditions, although this did not dampen the spirits of the crowds that turned out to witness the passing of an era. *John Fozard collection*

Left A desperately sad sight indeed: Roberts car No 536, the last member of the class that had entered service on 11 April 1952, lies in Thomas Ward's yard in December 1960 being ripped apart after just over eight years' service to the city. *R. J. Wiseman*

Above This is not the very last night of tramway operation in Sheffield, but a 'last night' scene nonetheless. At South Road, Walkley, a variety of people have turned out to witness Rocker panel car No 55 becoming the last car to leave the terminus for ultimate withdrawal. It is early on 8 April 1956 and buses will take over the Walkley-Intake service later in the day. Similar scenes would become more and more common over the next four years as one of the finest tramway systems in the United Kingdom declined. *A. K. Terry*

INDEX OF LOCATIONS